More praise for
Killing Giants

"For Method, taking on Big Soap means moving fast, fighting dirty, and changing the game by flipping the giants' strengths against them. Now you have the playbook."

—ERIC RYAN, COFOUNDER OF METHOD

"Stephen Denny has written a book for business leaders who compete with giants every day, offering brilliant examples of how to turn weaknesses into strengths."

—MARTIN ST. GEORGE, SENIOR VICE PRESIDENT OF
MARKETING AND COMMERCIAL STRATEGY, JETBLUE

"Denny cuts through the fat and gets into muscle. No models, no fluff, no disclaimer—just hard-hitting success stories and lessons learned. Denny reverse-engineers some true giant-slayings and leaves you with actionable insights. Read if you're looking to do the impossible."

—RICK DARNABY, FORMER REGIONAL PRESIDENT (EUROPE) OF MOTOROLA
AND FORMER CEO OF MONSANTO CANADA, INC.

"As we challenge ourselves each day to do more with less, *Killing Giants* provides a valuable resource, describing one brilliant marketing move after another, and identifying successful strategies for toppling our larger competitors."

—FRANCES ALLEN, EXECUTIVE VICE PRESIDENT AND
CHIEF MARKETING OFFICER, DENNY'S CORPORATION

"Creativity is a tool so powerful that industry giants quake in its presence. In *Killing Giants*, Stephen Denny shows us creative business thinking at its best. Provocative and invigorating."

—RICHARD HINSON, FORMER PRESIDENT AND GENERAL MANAGER, SEARLE CANADA

"You hold in your hands an insider's account of how real advantage-makers win. These movers and shakers disrupt the giants in their industries, and Denny does a marvelous job revealing how, and how you can, too."

—STEVEN FEINBERG, PhD, AUTHOR OF *THE ADVANTAGE-MAKERS*

"The ten strategies in *Killing Giants* offer any business a comprehensive approach for dealing with the new normal. Denny clearly and succinctly lays out stories and lessons learned from a broad range of companies. If you want to build a new company in today's environment, or reinvent an existing business, *Killing Giants* is a great place to start."

—DAMIEN LAMENDOLA, CEO OF WELLDYNE

KILLING
GIANTS

KILLING
GIANTS

10 STRATEGIES TO TOPPLE
THE GOLIATH IN YOUR INDUSTRY

STEPHEN DENNY

PORTFOLIO / PENGUIN

PORTFOLIO/PENGUIN
Published by the Penguin Group
Penguin Group (USA) Inc., 375 Hudson Street,
New York, New York 10014, U.S.A.
Penguin Group (Canada), 90 Eglinton Avenue East,
Suite 700, Toronto, Ontario, Canada M4P 2Y3
(a division of Pearson Penguin Canada Inc.)
Penguin Books Ltd, 80 Strand, London WC2R 0RL, England
Penguin Ireland, 25 St. Stephen's Green, Dublin 2,
Ireland (a division of Penguin Books Ltd)
Penguin Books Australia Ltd, 250 Camberwell Road,
Camberwell, Victoria 3124, Australia
(a division of Pearson Australia Group Pty Ltd)
Penguin Books India Pvt Ltd, 11 Community Centre,
Panchsheel Park, New Delhi – 110 017, India
Penguin Group (NZ), 67 Apollo Drive, Rosedale, North Shore 0632,
New Zealand (a division of Pearson New Zealand Ltd)
Penguin Books (South Africa) (Pty) Ltd, 24 Sturdee Avenue,
Rosebank, Johannesburg 2196, South Africa

Penguin Books Ltd, Registered Offices:
80 Strand, London WC2R 0RL, England

First published in 2011 by Portfolio/Penguin,
a member of Penguin Group (USA) Inc.

1 3 5 7 9 10 8 6 4 2

LIBRARY OF CONGRESS CATALOGING IN PUBLICATION DATA
Denny, Stephen, 1962–
Killing giants : 10 strategies to topple the Goliath in your industry/Stephen Denny.
p. cm.
Includes index.
ISBN 978-1-59184-383-2
1. Marketing. 2. Strategic planning. I. Title.
HF5415.D457 2011
658.8'02—dc22
2010043591

Printed in the United States of America
Set in ITC Slimbach Book
Designed by Sabrina Bowers

TO NICHOLAS AND ALEXANDER,
IN HOPES THAT WHICHEVER THIRD WAY YOU CHOOSE PROVES TO BE
EFFORTLESS, NO MATTER HOW STEEP THE CLIMB.

Contents

KILLING
GIANTS

INTRODUCTION: *On Killing Giants*

We've all experienced the harsh reality of the Monday morning budget meeting, where department heads from all over the company have assembled at nine o'clock sharp in the boardroom, nervously fingering their budget decks, while you wait your turn to demonstrate the depth of your team's analysis and the cunning of its execution to your thankful management and admiring peers—only to have it all thrown out the window. Your budget has been cut. Your revenue target hasn't. You need to pick the two people from your five-person team whom you can live without. The layoffs aren't certain yet, but think about it. Let it hang over your head for the rest of the day. That lingering sense of dread should help you focus on rolling the boulder uphill today.

This isn't the first time this has happened in your career. Your boss undoubtedly had a similar meeting at eight, where his boss told him that he, too, would need to decide which budgets to ax and which air hoses to pinch off.

I'm a believer in questioning the givens. But at this moment, you wisely decide not to question the given of your newly slashed budget lest you become part of the cost savings instead of an

1

active member of the solution committee. You also conclude that now would be a poor time to launch a palace coup and try to change the face of your company's structure, strategy, and go-to-market plans.

You are not a general on a battlefield. You are not the admiral of your own navy. You are a soldier in a foxhole, facing an enemy that spends more on postage than you do on marketing. And your ammunition has been halved. Sorry.

LET'S AGREE THAT THIS is a story you've probably lived through more than a few times. Your job description never actually spelled out the words, "Do the impossible, every day, fighting against competitors so big they could crush you without even hearing your last indignant squeal." This was one of those early "aha" moments you had in your first few months on the job. While this may be your reality, I have good news. This is not a reason to despair. We are all being asked to do more with less, just as we're all expected to take market share away from the massive competitors we face. While it may be difficult, it may also be a blessing in disguise.

Our choices under pressure define us in business and in life. Our need to work smarter with fewer resources against long odds isn't dependent on the state of the economy or on any sense of stability you *think* you have in your industry.

Less is the new normal.

Less defines how consumers and businesses are thinking about consuming. Everyone is rethinking their choices, and they look at what they choose to buy through very different eyes than they did a few short years ago. This isn't going to change anytime soon, so the faster we adapt to the new world, the happier and more prosperous we'll be. Not adapting—or shutting our eyes and pretending that the familiar patterns will reemerge after the dust settles—is dangerous, because the giants we face every day will kill us if they can.

The New Normal

"There's a fundamental shift taking place in America." Paul Leinberger is the executive vice president of The Futures Company (formerly Yankelovich) and is a recognized authority on consumer sentiment tracking. "There have only been three of these major shifts since the Second World War," he tells me. "There was an Era of New Frontiers after the war with the economy growing but with the Great Depression still in their heads. Then, we had a time of expanding expectations. That era ran through a few major recessions. This Era of Indulgence showed us the powerful rise of true brands."

Then came 2007. The Era of Indulgence came to a halt faster than a leased BMW hitting a telephone pole. Emerging from the Great Recession, we're now entering what Leinberger calls the Era of Consequences. "One of the lessons of the recession is that we were living beyond our means," Leinberger continued. "We're now learning—some more painfully than others—that we need to think about every purchase. On the other side of the coin is that marketers need to speak to these new customers differently."

If you were hoping that this new Era of Consequences was simply a case of temporary frugality, you have my sympathies. It isn't. Its causes are complex and deep-seated, and the effects will be long lasting. "My clients say, Paul, when we get out of this, people will go back to the way it was, right?" He leans closer. "They don't like to hear me tell them that no, things will never be the same. You are not dealing with the same consumer you were a few years ago. The world of Hummers is gone, and not just for a little while—they're gone forever." Consumers no longer act as though it's all about "me" anymore. The pain is shared and we receive mutual support from those around us. It's about me, but also my family, my community, and my planet.

In the place of Hummers and lavish personal spending, consider an era of smart consumerism. Conspicuous consumption has given way to consumers bragging to their friends that they've made good choices. Importantly, there's an increased degree of vigilance to this new feeling of smart consumerism. The definition of value has become more complex. It's not that people won't spend money—we will—but the way that we look at everything we do has changed.

When consumers do choose to spend, they now view all purchases as competing for the same funds. "It's no longer Cadillac versus Lexus," Leinberger said. "It's 'Should I buy a car at all? Maybe I'll save for my child's education or fix my house up instead.'" All product categories must now compete for our dollars against all others.

On the job, things have changed as well. The effects of the economic meltdown continue to manifest themselves in a number of unpleasant ways, many of which affect each of us in our professional pursuits. According to Leinberger's research, a full 42 percent of consumers feel anxious when they leave their home in the morning about whether they will still have a job when they come home that night. Once a word used only to describe environmental responsibility, increasingly we hear employees demanding "social sustainability" in their workplaces—a sustainable business model with an increased focus on fairness, a workplace free from fear.

Hiring managers now speak of the desire to find "generalists"—people who can wear multiple hats—ostensibly because each employee must do tasks once done by teams of specialists. The darker underside of this trend is that companies no longer want to be reliant on a hard-to-replace specialist, preferring to hire interchangeable cogs that can be replaced with little risk. Not a terribly comforting thought.

When we look at how corporations view this new age of consumption, we see more of the same. IT spending and other capital expenditures are delayed, with companies preferring to make do with the systems they have in place for one more year, then another. A quick scan of the reports monitoring technology purchases by corporations shows us the widespread desire to lengthen the deployed life of equipment while minimizing upgrades. When equipment or software is to be purchased, buyers are looking for paybacks within one budget cycle. And any and all options for reducing costs—including fixed head count in favor of outsourcing—are on the table.

None of this means that the world has come to an end. All of it means that the conditions we've taken for granted for many, many years no longer apply.

We need to change how we think, how we talk to our consumers, and how we choose to spend the reduced dollars we have in our care. The Era of Consequences is also the Age of Working Smarter.

The Nature of Competition and the Role of the Underdog

We love it when giants fall. It's part of our collective social consciousness. We build up heroes and, once they reach a certain plateau of success over a period of time, we tire of them. We love underdogs and want to see an upset.

This is an advantage in many instances for anyone competing against a giant. While you grapple with their built-in authority and gravitas, there's a force in the background that works to your advantage. We all like "new." We are quick to share—with our friends, peers, and even our competitors—when we know things that they don't. If we're open to suggestion and want to learn what others may not know, it also means we're open to options apart from what the industry giant is offering. Your "new" can beat their "authority."

This wrinkle entitles us to nothing, though. It means the door is open to our offer, but in no way does it suggest that we have an advantage. We need to earn what we take from giants with very smart, proactive strategic thinking and tactical execution. If we do nothing, inertia sets in and the giant's gravitational pull eventually takes our customer base away. But when we act, the door opens wider. The more we do that taps the buyer's decision triggers—that appeals to their desire for exclusivity, for the "newer new" and the psychological advantages that conveys—the more they're willing to listen.

Success can breed success for the careful.

The Power of Thinking Tools: The Story as Competitive Advantage

So how do we lever this door open? How do we shorten the learning curve from typical trial and error to starting with a shorter list of options?

We use stories because we pay attention to them where lessons would leave us cold. Stories form a cultural bond between us and have been our primary means of transmitting information on "how to live" since we descended from the trees and sat around campfires at night.

There is far more to stories than entertainment. Archetypal psychology focuses on stories and myths that are reflected in the patterns of our lives. Brain science tells us that stories connect us to concrete experience rather than abstract ideas. We psychologically process narrative differently than we do simple factual evidence. Dr. Norman Holland, an expert in the study of how the brain reacts when under the influence of a compelling story and a former professor at the University of Florida, explained to me that, "We have good psychological evidence that people believe stories momentarily, even when the stories cast doubt on something they know perfectly well is true." Our ability to use "thinking tools"—stories that allow us to put ourselves in the shoes of another and try their experiences on to see if they fit our realities—offers a quicker route to our goals. This is a skill we all need to develop: the ability to put on adaptive personas as a means to discovering new approaches to old problems. I'll take you on this path in *Killing Giants* by exposing you to businesses that may have nothing to do with what you do today but whose stories feature people facing very similar problems.

What connects all of us—from those giant-killers profiled here to the rest of us, working hard every day to overcome the giants we face—is that we all encounter similar challenges. We are dealing with real constraints—constraints of budgets, manpower, and time.

The good news is that constraints aren't a curse.

They're ammunition.

Constraints and Why They Help— Rather Than Hurt—Us

How will we scale this vertical wall and fight the giant on top of it? The change we are faced with is a constraint—in this case, one of fewer resources. We don't have the budget or head count we once had. We need to do more with less.

So why is this good news?

Constraints force us to make choices. Constraints make us

think harder. But they also give force, focus, and structure to our creativity. It's too easy to throw money at problems. That's what giants do every day. They spend money instead of time. You don't have the luxury of considering this option, and frankly, as you'll see, this is actually a good thing. You're going to have to work harder to get to where you're going, but the thinking and execution behind your efforts will have longer lasting, more powerful effects than would ever have resulted from a quick hand-off to some agency. It will stick, in other words. It will make more sense to everyone, including you.

Let me give you a quick example of the impact of constraints on your thinking. Let's pick a product. We're going to design a child's car seat. We'll go through three examples to get you going.

First, take out your pen and your notepad and reimagine the car seat. Go.

Whenever you've got something, just raise your hand.

If you're like most people, you looked at the page with a mix of confusion and bewilderment for a few moments and then doodled for a few more. It's practically impossible to just "re-create" something out of thin air. If you found this exercise difficult, you're not alone.

Now, take your pen and reimagine the car seat. One more thing: You've got exactly ten seconds. Go.

Again, if you're like most people, you jumped a few inches out of your seat when I said "go." But by the end of ten seconds, you'd probably actually written a couple of things down. And they were better than the doodles you did above. We introduced a constraint: the constraint of time. You had to make decisions, and you did.

Take your pen one last time and reimagine the car seat. One more bit of information you need before you start: Design this car seat with older parents in mind—parents with bad backs.

I probably didn't even have to say go. You were off and running. You had ideas, one after the other. The seat can swivel ninety degrees, it can run on a rail across the backseat so that it's easy to put the child in at either door, it's got a clip that's secure but easy to use so putting the seat in and taking it out doesn't take so much work, and so on. The constraint introduced here is very organic: the intended customer and all the things we associate with them—older parents with their creaking backs. Now, you had the opportunity to put your mind into a particular frame and work inside a fully realized constraint.

Why do constraints help? Perhaps we're all just better art critics than artists. Perhaps we need that first moment of inspiration and the rest takes on a life of its own.

You're dealing with a constraint of resources now—people and money—which means you need to do more with less. You need levers, tools that can act as force multipliers, to make up the difference. These thinking tools are what make competing against giants possible.

About Killing Giants

Once upon a time in late 2006, a former colleague of mine wrote me an e-mail out of the blue. I hadn't heard from her since our time working together a few years before, but she said that she was reading my blog and finding it useful. She mentioned that she was working for a mid-tier consumer electronics brand stuck, as she called it, "between two giants." I've spent a sizable part of my career in this same situation in one form or another. Even during my years working at $86 billion Sony Electronics, I faced a giant—in tiny little TDK, a specialty magnet manufacturer. TDK was a fraction of our size when viewed at the parent company level, but it was our biggest competitor in audiotape and videotape. This disparity in size between competitors served to illustrate what has become an important distinction as my thinking on the competitive structures within industries evolved: Who the giant is in any particular situation comes down to relative strengths that often aren't apparent at first glance. I started typing a reply to her note with a few ideas off the top of my head and soon realized my e-mail had run to more than five hundred words and counting. And I was just getting started. I thought it would be rude to hit Send at this point (imagine getting this on a BlackBerry!) so I saved the work-in-progress to the desktop, sent her a one-line reply, and went on with my day.

That five-hundred-word clip sat there for weeks, staring at me from my desktop. I finally turned it into a blog post in January 2007, calling it "Killing Giants, Part 1." Understand I didn't know there was a part two to be written at this point. The name generated itself, for some reason. What became the second part was my first contribution to MarketingProfs' Daily Fix blog, followed by a part three on my own blog later. The number of ideas waxed and waned over time, from nine to twelve at any given time. I pushed and pulled at these ideas over the course of the following year, using them in my consulting work and firetesting them with friends launching their own companies. They held up. I kept them around. They refused to die.

Each business leader I interviewed in *Killing Giants*—more than seventy—gravitated to this universal idea. Everyone understands fighting a giant. Their stories are very powerful, as you'll see. Some are fighting giants that dwarf them in size. Others had even bigger challenges, fighting calcified ideas, bureaucratic constraints, and other kinds of "giants."

And while *Killing Giants*, without reservation, is a business book, it holds a deeper promise: that fighting and defeating giants, however large and imposing, is not only possible but noble. It isn't a question of money. It's a matter of progress and change for the better.

KILLING GIANTS IS FOR every businessperson facing an industry colossus. Giant-killers work in marketing, sales, operations, finance, strategy, the C-suite, and the front lines. They have titles like manager, director, vice president, or chief marketing officer. They may own their own business or be pitching angel investors for the funding to launch one. They may work for a multi-billion dollar global behemoth, facing a competitor that dwarfs even them. To be clear, this isn't always about small companies fighting big ones, although this is most common. There are some very nimble big companies and there are stodgy bureaucracies to be found in the smallest organizations that would suffocate the best ideas. Sometimes the giant is much smaller than you are, a well-entrenched niche player, while you are a tiny division of a global enterprise, looking to carve some business out for yourselves with corporate looking over your shoulder. Often it's the story of a start-up fighting against an industry incumbent.

Giants, in other words, come in all shapes and sizes, as do the Davids that slay them. This is a question of smarts versus brawn. And that brings us to the point. What connects each is a desire to do the impossible, every day: kill the giant in their industry.

What It Is
(and What It Isn't)

The stories collected here and the "thinking tools" we can extract from them will give us a wide assortment of new ways to look at our challenges. I've presented ten strategies here—ten ideas—illustrating each with a handful of stories approaching them from different angles. We can view a single idea from multiple perspectives and interpret each against our own reality. We can try on these "alternative selves" to see if these stories help us think through our problems.

The ten chapters that follow describe strategies that can wrong-foot the giant in your industry. I know this for two good reasons. First, others have gone before us. The examples in each chapter animate how smart companies have approached complex problems and emerged with sustainable footholds against entrenched competitors. Second, I've employed many of these strategies myself (and lived to write the book!), so I've seen them work from the inside out.

You can start on page one of *Killing Giants* and make your way through its entirety as you fly across the Pacific. You can also chip away at it a chapter or a story at whim. Nothing says you can't pick a chapter that makes sense to read now and catch others as they become useful. I've designed it to be a nonlinear read. We work in a nonlinear world, and I won't force a structure on you that doesn't fit your work style.

More important, I hope you'll quickly discard those chapters that don't meet your needs. This allows you to focus your attention on those that do. When you find a tool that fits your circumstances, apply it rigorously. Work through it, understanding the essential point of the story and applying it to your situation. My role is to set the idea in motion—yours is to bring it to life.

Let's also be clear about what *Killing Giants* isn't. This is not a loose compendium of war stories. It isn't a census-level analysis of industry analytics with a resulting trend line that provides a few interesting insights. I've avoided writing "case studies" here; instead, I offer stories, as verbatim as possible, straight from the participants. Many, if not most, of these stories have not been told before. And, heaven forbid, *Killing Giants* is not about "advice." Advice is overrated. Advice, when given from some lofty perch, tends to shine a bright spotlight on all the good moves one recalls (while one conveniently forgets the nasty parts). Advice is specific to place, time, and circumstance, so what worked for the Iconoclast isn't, in all likelihood, going to work for you. I wish it were that easy, but it isn't.

None of these strategies is a silver bullet. All require work. But there are nuggets of collected wisdom from some of industry's most brilliant and accomplished businesspeople, individuals who have overcome obstacles very similar, at heart, to the ones you face today. Listen carefully to what they are saying here. Ask questions of yourself before hurling conclusions out into space. None of these is a "fire and forget" instant-win tactic. Each requires significant thought and analysis to determine what makes the most sense for you, today, versus your set of competitors, and using those resources available to you.

Also, understand I've anointed no winners in this book, preferring to recognize good work wherever it serves to teach a valuable lesson. Some of the companies profiled in *Killing Giants* have been acquired, some have gone out of business, and more will likely be gone in ten years' time. Not a problem. What they did is worth discussing and emulating if and when it makes sense for your business.

Not all strategies will work for you. More than one will, though.

Structure and Content

Each chapter is divided into three components. First, I describe the strategy. Then, **The Stories** reveal how each strategy played out under live fire. Some companies featured in these stories are iconic, some are relatively unknown. Not all battles are fought and won on the cover of *Fortune* magazine. **The Take-Aways** provide bullet-point-level summaries of the key ideas in each chapter.

The first rule tells us never to fight the giant on its home turf. Instead, bring it out over the **Thin Ice** of your own choosing. This is a war of nuance, taking advantage of your ability to hijack the conversation and play in areas where the giant has little to gain and less time to do it. Pick a fight in a place where they can't beat you and you'll often find the giant has no interest in fighting at all.

Speed kills giants. You are quicker and more maneuverable than a market leader painted into a corner of its own success. Speed cultures can be fostered within any organization at any level. It's never a matter of cutting corners, either—it's a question of rapid alignment, of ending the internal debate, and of moving toward action, all while the giant is still arranging its staff meetings.

Let the giant spend millions to generate interest and traffic—concentrate on **Winning in the Last Three Feet,** intercepting those same customers at the very moment they're primed and ready to buy. Awareness and interest doesn't always equal conversion. Smart brands find ways to leverage other people's investments.

And while we're talking about fighting, let's acknowledge that life isn't fair—so why not start **Fighting Dirty**? Pick the fight you can win. The right mismatch can be devastating to even the best competitive products. And no one said you had to fight by the giant's rules anyway.

Eat the Bug teaches us that doing the unthinkable is a strategy the giant can't imitate. Giants can't do what you can because their systems, structures, brands, and even worldviews preclude them from going where you can thrive. It's all about upping the ante in a game the giant doesn't even want to be playing.

Make the math hurt. **Inconvenient Truths** speak to pricing strategies that go far beyond the dreaded "What will it take to get your business?" line of logic. Where pricing is often relegated to the mechanics on the team, we will explore how to throw the psychological switch that turns on the "buy button" in your customer's head—and sends your competition to the "no sale" side of the ledger.

Don't fit in and be polite. Force people to make a choice. So go ahead and **Polarize on Purpose.** We'll explore how several brands have drawn attention to their defining features and succeeded by being very different. This is a chapter dedicated to the art of distillation. Forcing your customer to make meaningful choices can create the contrast that separates you from the giants.

Faster, nimbler brands with confidence and swagger can **Seize the Microphone** in their industries and dominate the conversation. You might be the only one talking to your customers in the room, you might be the only one anticipating their next burning need, and you might be the only one showing them how to pursue their passion.

Putting **All the Wood Behind the Arrow(s)** means not trying to win everywhere—it means you have to resoundingly win in a few key areas. But being an expert in only one area isn't enough. As you'll see, being one-dimensional is a losing game. So pick your spot(s) and win at the point(s) of your choosing.

When you're unquestionably better at what you do, seize the day. **Show Your Teeth.** Pursue your competitive advantage vigorously with every means you have. Hammer away at the giant's weaknesses with boring consistency and be the competitor they just don't want to face.

Remember that innovation always comes from elsewhere. You will read stories from industries that have nothing to do with you. Read them anyway. Ask yourself how you'd apply these foreign lessons to your own situation. Do this as a mental exercise. If you've ever asked yourself, "What would an anthropologist say about the customer behavior in my market?" or,

"What would a Mafia don tell me to do about this sales problem?" then do the same here. How does Jim Koch's brilliant positioning of Samuel Adams beer relate to my SaaS (Software as a Service) brand? What insights from Bob Parsons and Go Daddy can I apply to my apparel line? Stretch.

IT WILL FEEL LIKE a complete waste of time right up until the moment an unexpected insight changes everything.

CHAPTER ONE: *Thin Ice*

It's time to go where giants fear to tread.

Thin Ice is dangerous to companies who are too big to venture far from the relative safety of familiar ground. The giant's weight shifts and the ice cracks and groans underneath its feet. It's dangerous out here. Better to retreat than to risk everything.

But you know the ice can support your weight. You made this patch of ice in the first place. So taunt the giant all you want.

When we create our own **Thin Ice,** we change the environment to suit our needs. We move the public dialogue to a place where the giant is unprepared to go. Rather than risk the loss of face that will come from such a fight, the giant will likely choose to simply not fight at all.

There are 2 kinds of warfare: asymmetrical and stupid.

—DR. CONRAD CRANE, DIRECTOR OF THE U.S. ARMY HISTORICAL SOCIETY AND AUTHOR OF THE U.S. ARMY/MARINE CORPS COUNTERINSURGENCY FIELD MANUAL

"All commanders are looking for an edge. No commander goes out and says, 'I'm going to fight you just the way you expect me to.'" Dr. Conrad Crane of the U.S. War College in Carlisle, Pennsylvania, was the lead author of the current counterinsurgency doctrine for General David Petraeus and thus discusses competitive strategy on a more consequential level than any business discussion will ever cover. But having the lead author of the U.S. doctrine on counterinsurgency weighing in on Mao Zedong's theory of protracted warfare provides us with a number of insights not commonly covered in lighter reading material.

"You always look for a way of warfare that gives you an edge over your adversary," he explained. "As Americans, we rely on airpower and firepower. That's our asymmetric edge. Mao looked at time and space. He said, 'I'm going to set up a procedure where I can create a long war and wear the other guy down.'"

Crane identified the three parts of Mao's theory of protracted war—guerilla warfare—starting with creating defendable ground. "Mao's first phase is setting up bases and building strength," Crane said. "He retreated far back into the Chinese hinterland to set up his bases. You build up your strength among the people." Once you've established a safe haven—a sanctuary—you can use as a launching pad for future attacks, the second phase begins. "When you're strong enough for military action, you begin your guerilla attacks. You nip at their heels." The war of attrition—leveraging the advantages of time and space—creates gaps in the enemy's resources and morale. "Eventually, the time will come when the correlation of forces swings in your favor and then you go to major conventional operations to overwhelm your foe." The third phase is the knockout blow.

Mao's unique contribution to this body of work is unmistakable, and his thoughts on insurgent struggle have influenced indigenous struggles since the 1930s. Importantly, Mao's doctrine encompasses flexibility. Setbacks are understood and accounted for. "If you move to conventional combat too fast and you're defeated, you can go back to guerilla warfare." There is no timetable for the revolution. It happens when the conditions are right.

Mao's ideas about defendable ground, flexibility in thinking, and winning the hearts and minds of the people still apply today.

"One of the big things that helped us in Anbar Province was that Al-Qaeda's thinking was too inflexible in shaping its program to the needs of the people. Eventually, the people turned against them. Al-Qaeda antagonized the people more than they helped them. You've got to be able to get support from the people you need on your side."

Crane's counterinsurgency doctrine has shaped how U.S. forces are conducting their efforts in Iraq and Afghanistan today, but it took Professor Ian MacMillan's course in Entrepreneurial Management at Wharton to drive these concepts home for me. He opened the class with a deep analysis of Mao's 1937 treatise entitled *On Guerilla Warfare*, where the parallels with bootstrapping a start-up are hard to miss upon reflection. MacMillan told us that he'd fail one out of four of us on principle, just to get us used to start-up life, which focused the attention of the average second-year graduate student in his last trimester like a laser.

The first rule of guerilla warfare is ensuring you have the strategic insulation necessary to weather the political and military uncertainties of a newly developing movement—defendable ground as well as both stockpiled and self-generating surplus resources. In addition, Dr. MacMillan taught us about the art of maneuverability, of becoming comfortable with the fluidity of the lines of engagement and the discipline to only engage the enemy under conditions that suit you. These are skills that separate successful revolutionaries from dead ones.

Dr. Crane's and Dr. MacMillan's teachings are the touchstones of those nimble brands that choose to fight against giants on a daily basis.

The idea of strategic insulation and defendable ground suggests that you can find a place where a giant is reluctant to go. What does this mean in a life of business? One would be forgiven for concluding that there are few areas truly beyond the reach of a giant, with acquisition of either intellectual property or entire competitors a relatively painless decision for well-financed competitors. But the reality is that giants, many times for cultural reasons alone, don't often take this step. Why? Because giants are busy and arrogant. Giants have other fights to fight. When a smart guerilla company enjoys strategic insulation and puts the giant at a relative disadvantage, the giant very often walks away, preferring to deal with whatever else is on their to-do list.

Thin Ice is about hijacking the conversation, making the giant compete on ground where its size and relative strength no longer matter. To Mao, this was time and space. To Dr. Crane and his counterinsurgency doctrine, this is removing the enemy's sanctuaries—whether they are geographic, technological, or intellectual.

The Politics of Identity: Black Like Me

At that time, being black wasn't something you shouted about. But now, [Mashaba] tapped into all of that identity. He understood the psyche of the people he was marketing to. He was treating the black market like a market. This brand was theirs.

—MOKY MAKURA, NIGERIAN ENTREPRENEUR AND
TELEVISION PERSONALITY

Anyone raising himself on the streets from an early age as a professional gambler would develop a finely honed sense for the "tells" of a market. The nonverbal signals of the black township communities in apartheid-era South Africa must have been deafening to Herman Mashaba, but if his innate skill at understanding people was clear, his entrée into the world of business was anything but obvious.

"I got into business by pure accident," Mashaba told me. "The second year of my studies, one morning in April, the university was surrounded by the police at six in the morning and we were told to leave by noon the same day. That was the end of my academic career."

Leaving the university and returning to the townships, he worked a series of jobs as a salesman, selling insurance, table wear, and eventually cosmetics, all on commission. Each path, however, led to a dead end. "The people around me worked for white companies all their lives. Their white employer, whenever they wanted to get rid of them, they did. I looked for a way to be in charge of my own life." In cosmetics, Mashaba found the idea that would launch Black Like Me.

To fully understand the lessons of Black Like Me, one must appreciate the daily realities of a black businessman in apartheid South Africa. "In the first place, as black South Africans, we weren't South Africans," Mashaba explained. "For black people, in order to move around, you had to have a white employer who signed your ID on a monthly basis. I didn't have a white employer. To go into those (white) areas every day was quite risky. We had police all over the townships. I learned about ducking and diving from the police every day to avoid the road blocks. Fortunately, I managed to outlast the system."

Mashaba's break came in 1984. He grasped that the hair-care products he was selling on commission were relatively easy to manufacture. More important, unlike selling insurance or tableware, cosmetics were consumable products with predictable repurchase cycles. Mashaba carefully approached a white colleague with a manufacturing background with the idea of

launching a new brand. A subsequent meeting with a successful black financier led to the launch of the new company. They
began manufacturing in 1985 in a two-hundred-square-meter
facility.

The defining feature of Mashaba's brand is its name. "We
decided to go for a name that was immediately recognizable. As
soon as we came up with Black Like Me, I said this is the name."
This was a risky choice at the time. The company was positioned
from its outset as being an extension of the black community of
the townships. "We positioned Black Like Me to the black South
Africans as, 'This is your company.' It was benefiting the people.
There was a strong sense of belonging."

This was a new experience to many in the South African black
community. "Typically, the people who marketed were white people selling products—they were pushing a product into the black
market—where Mashaba actually created a brand that seemed to
understand where the market came from," Nigerian entrepreneur
and television personality Moky Makura told me. As to how Black
Like Me took root in the oppressive days of apartheid, Makura
explained, "Understand the South African black people. They are
always quick to put on a concert, they have a lot of celebrities and
performers, they're quick to celebrate with a song and a dance.
A lot of people don't have money, so they entertain themselves.
Life was miserable under apartheid. This was his understanding
of what life was like. Going down this entertainment path wasn't
so much about what the brand was about, it was more about
understanding what this market wanted."

While entertainment was a large part of the brand's connection with the community, the company also knew the realities of
life for its core market. Mashaba's vision extended beyond live
events to teaching his township customers how to best use his
grooming products through television advertising, a stark departure from the kind of afterthought marketing done to date for this
underserved market. He also positioned Black Like Me as a brand

synonymous with hope. "The police were killing our people all over the townships," Mashaba said. "We sponsored events to help families afford funerals. During Easter and festival seasons, we sponsored the helicopters and the reporters that people saw on television providing emergency services on the roads. This gave us massive exposure. It gave people the sense of belonging."

Above all, Black Like Me was dedicated to providing quality products at a discount to its township customer base. The brand always kept product sizes the same as its giant competitors but offered them at a 10 to 15 percent savings.

Herman Mashaba told me he wanted to be more than a consumer brand to his customer base. "We wanted Black Like Me to be the Coca-Cola of hair-care products. We always said that you could find Coca-Cola in the professional zones or the townships. People drink it whether they're rich or poor. We wanted to be the Coca-Cola of hair-care products. And now we're one of the largest hair-care products in all of Africa."

What enduring lessons can we take away from Black Like Me?

- **YOU DON'T NEED TO EXPLAIN WHO BLACK LIKE ME IS FOR.** The brand name instantly conveys a story of identity, pride, belonging, and shared experience. It's iconic and unforgettable. It doesn't blend in—and if you're a black South African, that matters.

- **WE PREFER TO DO BUSINESS WITH PEOPLE WE KNOW AND LIKE.** The social psychology of interpersonal influence supports the idea that similarity and "liking" drive preference and purchase decisions. All things being equal, we go with people "like us"—and in Black Like Me's case, things weren't equal at all.

- **UNDERSTANDING YOUR MARKET MEANS MORE THAN JUST ENTERTAINING THEM.** We need context and detail. To prove that "you" are one of "us," you need to show us that you understand something deeper than what makes us happy. You need to understand what motivates and concerns us. This is a connection on a deeper level than many brands are able to operate.

- **CONSTRAINTS DEFINE BRANDS.** Herman Mashaba didn't just carve out a niche for his company by going head-to-head against the usual suspects in the hair-care industry. He managed to do so as a black South African during apartheid. This really wasn't supposed to happen. He didn't buck the system, either. He worked within its confines (most of the time) and dodged when he needed to dodge. In the end, he outlasted the system.

Black Like Me provides a blueprint for connecting with a market defined by a shared sense of identity. The black community in apartheid South Africa was unified in its oppression and its shared experiences living under institutional racism. This pressure built a sense of identity that Herman Mashaba tapped into, providing a product, a brand, and an experience that his market identified with. Black Like Me is an important example of giant killing—not only did he outmaneuver the giants in hair-care products, he managed to outwit the apartheid system designed to stop people like him from being successful in the first place.

The Branding of Nationality: Baidu

Clearly Baidu has always sought to position itself as the local champion, with greater insight into the grammatical and cultural subtleties of the Chinese language—something that goes over well with Chinese audiences, who flatter themselves to think that Chinese is an especially complex language.

—KAISER KUO, FORMER BUREAU CHIEF OF RED HERRING'S BEIJING
OFFICE AND CHINA INTERNET INDUSTRY WATCHER

Baidu has always played the role of the brash local champion in China's Internet search market, but aside from the brand's feature set and technical merits, its genius is apparent in how it plays to its market's cultural bias: Baidu is just "more Chinese" than Google. And it's not shy about saying it—loudly, clearly, and often.

Baidu evolved into a stand-alone search engine after originally being a behind-the-scenes provider to several of China's major portals, including Sina.com and Sohu.com. Founder Robin Li explained that his change in strategy came as a result of the stark realization that as an OEM supplier to other consumer-facing portals he would only be able to compete on price. "During the summer of 2001," he recalled, "the Internet industry was in a difficult time, and we gradually realized that this company can't survive if we stick with the back-end technology provider thing. I made the decision to switch gears and become a consumer-oriented search site. The risk is that you basically start to compete against every single one of your customers . . . but if we don't do that, I don't see the future of this company." Li went on to describe the differences between being a back-end supplier and one that has to fight for consumer mind-share each and every day. "When you are a back-end tech provider, you are selling a commodity. You have to be as good as everyone else on the market. When you are a front-end consumer-oriented service, you have to be better—you have to be significantly better—than your competition, because you are a latecomer."

His early mover advantage proved to be a defining move, as competitors who followed in his footsteps quickly fell behind. As a search engine provider, Baidu has shown a clear under-standing of the unique nature of the China market, with a will-ingness to swim in waters that others have found a bit too risky. Music has long dominated online activity in China, and while the company has never released numbers that divulge the search volume for MP3 downloads, many estimates suggest that music accounts for more than 50 percent of all Internet searches in the country. Baidu also realized that Chinese Internet users have a greater tolerance for paid search results mixing with organic results. They have taken advantage of this, blurring the distinc-tion between both kinds of results, without the public backlash one would expect in the American market.

Baidu's emergence as a consumer-facing search company also coincided with the blooming of Internet use in China, creating an environment conducive for stand-alone search products. The company also benefited from market saturation in the top urban cities: Beijing, Shanghai, Guangzhou, and Shen-zhen had Internet penetration above 70 percent, while the rest of the country was in the 25 percent range. So while the urban technorati had some degree of comfort with "early adopter" brands like Google, the late-adopting rural and second-tier city users new to the Internet quickly gravitated to this more familiar local brand, whose name they could spell, whose marketing they'd seen, and whose products made sense to them right away.

As China came online, Baidu found itself in the right place at the right time—and with the right message. "Baidu's marketing has clearly helped, in part because they've been able to dominate the narrative without real reply from Google." Kaiser Kuo is an expert in the China Internet industry and the former bureau chief of *Red Herring*'s Beijing office. "The 'We know Chinese better than those guys' message does seem to resonate," he explained. A quick survey of Baidu's early television advertising shows even to non-Chinese speakers how stark the company has drawn the contrast between itself as local cultural champion and the bumbling, Abe-Lincoln-esque "American" brand, awkwardly stumbling over simple phrases in Chinese while Baidu's hero cleverly reels off a series of local dialect tongue-twisters. In the end, the onlookers celebrate Baidu's triumph and abandon the now ridiculed American icon, who falls to the ground vomiting blood—in case the spot's early subtlety didn't fully deliver the message.

Baidu has clearly solidified its image in the minds of Chinese Internet users as understanding Chinese better than its foreign rivals. "In informal polls I've done with Chinese users, I've found that people without much interest in the Internet beyond the Chinese-language Web are pretty convinced by this notion, and tend to use Baidu," Kuo related.

When I put this question to Li, I got a mixed response. "It's yet another misconception," he began. "We are a consumer-oriented company and we had to establish the perception of our brand." As for the actual marketing campaigns that defined the company's public persona, he again blurred the lines between the message intended for his investors prior to his IPO and the needs of his public, saying, "We came up with the idea that it's easy to convince them that Baidu understands Chinese better. We designed the strategy and came up with a number of marketing initiatives to tell the investors and the general public that Baidu has a better understanding of the Chinese language and the Chinese culture and that's why we're doing a better job." As the company spends roughly $20 million in advertising per year, and as their IPO is well behind them, we can assume that their branding is more focused on the general public at this point. The investors, we can assume, have been well taken care of.

Baidu's message clearly captured the imagination of the Chinese market, and the company is now enjoying a market share in the 60 to 70 percent range. There are several factors we can consider to explain this result. Against Baidu's very pointed "we speak Chinese better than Google does" campaign, Google remained quiet. Google's name was difficult for many to spell—some 70 percent of those surveyed, at one point—while Baidu uses a much simpler unmodified pinyin (Romanized Chinese) spelling. Apparently, Baidu *does* speak Chinese better than everybody else.

Baidu represents a clear case study in a local champion taking on—and soundly defeating—a globally dominant brand by playing by decidedly local rules, from a product lineup geared to local sensibilities to an aggressive marketing stance that, while mildly xenophobic, puts the highly visible outsider on the defensive.

What enduring lessons can we take away from Baidu?

- **ACT LIKE A LOCAL.** Understand what works here. Advertise a search engine? You see a little of this in the United States, but less than you'd see for the average midsize car, and rarely from U.S. market leader Google. But in China, it works. Calling in to small- and medium-size businesses asking for advertising? Unheard of in America. In China, it works.

- **WHAT ARGUMENT CAN YOUR GIANT NEVER WIN?** What is believable, relevant, and ownable? If your local market can't spell your name, and spelling your name is what they must do each and every time they use your product, you're at a decided disadvantage.

- **BAIDU IS LIKE US.** In any market, there are politics of identity. Sometimes that identity is racial, as with Black Like Me, and sometimes it is cultural and national and racial, like Baidu. Who says this is a bad way to position your brand? If your brand lives and breathes the same way your market does and "they" don't, you have a credible and authentic story to tell. Baidu's story is compelling for the average Internet user in rural China. It makes more sense.

- **AIM AT THE UNDERSERVED.** It's always seductive to position yourself "high and to the right." Many brands tend to default to premium positioning for the discerning consumer. Giant-killers love it when their competitors do this, because it leaves the other 90 percent of the market to them. There are always opportunities for brands who serve the underserved with a needed and quality solution.

Baidu gives us a vivid example of forcing a global giant to compete on ground where it can't easily win—the politics of cultural and national identity. Baidu did what the giant never thought to do, producing products that worked locally without worrying about whether it worked globally, and driving home the message in an unmistakable manner, with direct outreach to consumers that pitted Chinese stereotypes against American ones—with Baidu as the winner. As of this writing, Google's future in China is unclear, with the company redirecting search traffic to its uncensored Hong Kong site over allegations of the Chinese government's involvement in hacking the e-mail accounts of suspected dissidents. Baidu appears to be the last man standing.

. . .

BAIDU GIVES US A case study in how to successfully fight a global giant on your home turf.

Creating Experts and Anchor Points:
The Boston Beer Company

Could a giant do what we do? It's not impossible. It's difficult because it's not what they're good at. At a big company, this is a six- to twelve-month project . . . at the Boston Beer Company, this is our life's work. This is my life's work.

—JIM KOCH, FOUNDER OF THE BOSTON BEER COMPANY

"When I started the company, it became very clear to me that my real competition wasn't other brewers," Jim Koch explained to me one afternoon. "It was ignorance and apathy. It was people who didn't know about beer or care about beer." Since he quit his consulting career and launched the Boston Beer Company back in the early 1980s, Koch has been on a single-minded mission to change how the American consumer thinks about beer.

When you look back over the recent sweep of history, it's hard to remember a time when the most popular wine sold in the United States was the screw-top Thunderbird, aimed squarely at the corner wino, and when beer was a commoditized, mildly alcoholic drink not too different from soda pop. "Wine wasn't thought of as anything good—you drank it to get drunk," Koch recalled. "There was no real wine culture. Then, a handful of small California winemakers started making world-class wine, and they changed the understanding about wine. They looked at different varietals and producers. America became the equal of France at the high end of wines. That's the path that I knew

I needed to take beers." Koch continued, "We took an American staple that people took for granted and opened up this whole wide world of quality and variety and interestingness."

The craft explosion of the mid-1980s marked the beginning of what was to become a cultural change throughout the American beer market. Over the next three decades, Americans began to realize that beer could be a complex, quality product that stood on equal footing with not only its European counterparts but with the booming domestic wine industry. While still representing only a fraction of the total American beer market, the Boston Beer Company's signature Samuel Adams brand has seized the high ground of perceived quality and even garnered the surprising honor of becoming the largest American-owned brewery left, given the fact that market giants Anheuser-Busch and MillerCoors have both been acquired by international brewing conglomerates. But regardless of its relative size or market share, the brand has always been much happier to avoid any discussion of the competition. The giants still spill more beer than Jim Koch brews—and that's fine with him.

But if a giant wants to fight, Samuel Adams beer is willing to take the fight to the consumer and let them decide what they'd like to drink—and the combination the brand throws is a dangerous one to its mass-market competitors.

"Sam Adams is not a beginner's beer," Koch says to a group in his brewery in the first of a series of carefully crafted television advertisements. What a wonderfully loaded statement! What does it mean when your brand is not a "beginner's" brand? It suggests that something else is better for those who have no appreciation for a quality product like this. What goes through the mind of the consumer when they're faced with this choice? It suggests that if you don't like Sam Adams, you might just be a beginner yourself— and that you just might want to think about educating your palate. What happens when you stand at the bar with a Sam Adams in your hand and your friend has a mass-marketed soda-pop beer in his? Who has bragging rights? Notice that "Sam Adams is not a beginner's beer" says nothing directly disparaging about its competition. It has positioned itself vividly as an exclusive choice for only those people who consider themselves sophisticated beer drinkers. And we all like being thought of this way, don't we?

"The campaign works on many levels," Koch told me. "The beer drinker should understand that when they have a beer, it's not an alcoholic soda pop. It's the product of a ten-thousand-year-old human brewing tradition that began at the very start of civilization and one of the oldest arts in the world. It's something that has an enormous amount of variety and tradition and heritage, a big ability to deliver quality."

Boston Beer is serious about changing how Americans think about beer, and the company lives this mission every day by preaching and teaching what makes good beer. We can all recite slogans, but when we learn what "noble hops" are, or how to pour the perfect glass, or even how to brew beer in our kitchens, only then does beer culture get under our fingernails. The company launched a line of branded beer glasses with a series of proprietary features, from the shape of the lip to the wider "belly" of the glass to the laser-etched holes in the bottom to promote the uniform bubbles that make up the beer's distinctive head. Each employee is encouraged to brew at home—competing with their own company in a small sense, but more important, creating a brand expert capable of speaking with the credibility and authority that only first-person experience can impart. Each employee serves a stint at the factory to ensure that brewing beer on the macro level also gets into the blood. "Our mission is to educate people about beer and to change their attitudes about it so we can create customers for Sam Adams," Koch told me. "We had to educate people about what quality meant to people. It was outside their notion of what beer meant and could be. We had to expand this little box. Our people are trained on ingredients, almost all have home brewed, they know the ingredients and know what these ingredients do." This isn't the sort of culture that one casually bolts on, in other words.

When I asked Koch if one of his giants could wake up one day and roll over him, he said, "Could a giant do what we do? It's not impossible. It's difficult because it's not what they're good at. They're good at cost-effectively mass-producing beers that appeal to the mass market. They could make craft-styled beers if they put their minds to it. But it's hard for a big company to care about such specialized products. It's not outside their capabilities, but it's like McDonald's. Could McDonald's make filet mignon? Of course, but it's not the business they're in."

What enduring lessons can we take away from the Boston Beer Company?

- **SETTING OUT TO CHANGE HOW MILLIONS OF PEOPLE THINK ABOUT YOUR PRODUCT CATEGORY IS FUNDAMENTALLY DIFFERENT THAN DECIDING TO MAKE A GOOD PRODUCT.** When you set out to make the best lager (or olive oil, or VoIP solution), you're essentially out to please yourself. You're saying, I'm not going to stop until I think it's the best. But when you set out to change how everyone else thinks about your entire product category, you've signed up for much more. Instead of focusing on what you think, you're going to do whatever it takes to make your market think you're the best. This market-focused worldview quickly crushes any thoughts of myopic self-congratulation. The market is littered with brands that set out to do something well.

- **GIANTS HAVE DIFFERENT PROBLEMS THAN YOU DO.** As giants grow, their problems change. Often, this means that the focus on artisan quality begins to take a backseat to supply chains and logistics. Giants begin to reward those with the skills needed to supply their far-flung distribution outposts more than those who originally created and marketed the products. As problems evolve, focus shifts. A smart brand thrives in these areas; there is no need to contest ground already abandoned.

- **EXPERTS ARE MORE POWERFUL THAN EVANGELISTS.** Create an evangelist and they will cheer your product for as long as you have their attention. Create an expert and they'll talk about your product forever, for as long as their passion and their newfound skills make them happy. Learning the product's nuances and eccentricities firsthand is more powerful than any bolt-on training. Once it's under your team's fingernails, it's with them forever.

The Boston Beer Company shows us the path to a credible, authentic premium positioning versus an established giant. The product is superior, as judged by users. The vision is outwardly focused on changing how millions think. The people are committed in their missionary zeal and functional, artisanal expertise. And the message is so beautifully crafted to position its competitors over the very thin ice of expertise and exclusivity that it serves as a warning to category giants to stick to what they do best and not come any closer.

Key Takeaways

Thin Ice discusses how smart brands can change the dialogue in the market, forcing giants to compete on ground where their strengths are useless. If you can change the market's perception, begin a conversation that the giant can't join, or build a sense of identity where the giant feels out of place, you've put yourself where only you can thrive. Giants stay away for fear of looking foolish—and choose to fight again another day, somewhere else. What key takeaways can we extract from these stories?

What's the definition of "we"? Study the brands outlined in this chapter and you see case studies in identity— Black Like Me, Baidu, and the Boston Beer Company all have meaning to their respective fan bases. Herman Mashaba created a brand synonymous with the growing sense of identity in the townships of South Africa while Baidu was more Chinese than Google to Internet users in China. The Boston Beer Company came at this question from a different direction, seeking to create a movement and an identity within the American beer drinking market. Each is a standard bearer for their own chosen group.

Speaking like a local beats looking like a foreigner. Brands who have successfully targeted defined markets with a sense of collective identity not only understand the realities and dynamics of their markets better than the giants have, but prove this understanding with effective and appropriate communications strategies. Knowing is not enough. We must speak with a fluency that comes from living their life. If we can do this, we can position ourselves in a manner more credible and authentic than someone who simply puts on an accent for the camera.

Black Like Me knew that entertainment was an entrée to the lifestyle brand it wanted to be—and it also knew that entertainment wasn't enough, sponsoring education and social services that proved to its customer base that it knew their lives from the inside.

Baidu's product development and sales practices were very local—and very different from what their competitors did. They did business like a Chinese firm selling to Chinese customers, and those late adopters who flocked to the brand responded to this.

The Boston Beer Company's practice of employee indoctrination speaks to an almost ritual approach to creating experts. We must "get it under our fingernails" to understand the deep knowledge and nuance of our categories—things a giant will never bother to do.

Each "Thin Ice" brand is obvious in its own way. You don't have to explain who Black Like Me is for, do you? Likewise, Baidu made it clear that its competitor, "Google"—a name most search consumers in China can't spell—didn't speak Chinese or understand its subtleties and complexities as well as it did. The Boston Beer Company created its own niche and sought through its own actions to establish a new concept of what beer meant to the American public.

Each brand in this chapter is self-defining, which makes them hard to compete against, head to head, on their own terms. Their competitive insulation is in their very fabric.

Look to your defendable ground. Each of these three brands has been able to hold their defendable ground against the onslaughts of their respective giants because they have great competitive insulation—defendable ground—that is both unique and hard to replicate.

Black Like Me was embedded within the psyche of the black township communities, and everything they did and stood for reinforced their core message that "this is your brand." Baidu stated the obvious—that they were "more Chinese than the other guys" because it was an argument hard to resist, particularly when the competitive giant had a name most consumers couldn't spell. The Boston Beer Company could say "take pride in your beer" with confidence because it knew the giant couldn't fight on that ground—the ice was just too thin. In each case, our giant-killers positioned themselves in a manner that made it easy for them to attack and similarly easy for them to defend.

Giants are different from you, and what first made them successful may have nothing to do with what makes them successful as giants today. They have different problems, different strengths, and often a different focus than you have. You won't be able to find their blind spot ahead of time. You will have to create that blind spot for them with focus and positioning of your own.

CHAPTER TWO: *Speed*

Giants have a culture of process. You have a culture of speed.

They enter a first-phase evaluation. You launch a product.

They form a steering committee. You launch a second-generation product.

They form a "tiger team" to study your first-generation product while you ship your third-generation product.

They can't hit what they can't catch. Win on speed.

There's a hell of a lot happening at the same time . . . twenty people drilled to do the same thing, time in and time out. It's no good having three corners doing the wheel stop in 2.5 seconds and one doing it in 4.5 seconds. You all have to get drilled down to doing the exact same thing at the same time.

—OLE SCHACK, #2 MECHANIC AND FRONT LEFT WHEEL GUN MAN, RED BULL RACING'S FORMULA 1 TEAM

The Formula 1 racing administration passed down a rule in 2010 that eliminated refueling during pit stops, dramatically affecting both racing strategy and car design. The biggest impact of this rules change, however, was on the pit crews. All of a sudden, pit crew speed was important.

"Changing the four tires last year, you were never under pressure," Red Bull Racing's Ole Schack told me. "Last year, fuel was the limiting factor depending on your strategy. Maybe your car sat in the pit lane for eight seconds or ten seconds. Now, the limiting factor is how quick you can do it."

Red Bull's Formula 1 team management took this change very seriously. The team was sent to the UK's Olympic training facility for a summer, undergoing a series of hand-eye coordination diagnostics and training to determine who was best for which role in the twenty-person pit crew. Once the crews were selected, they drilled—Schack described his three-person team practicing swapping out front left tires 150 times a day, seven days a week—so that the economy of movement could be studied, optimized, and further refined to shave off ever-decreasing amounts of time. Processes were reengineered, such as the body angle of the gun man responsible for removing the nuts from a tire as the car approaches the pit. Obstruct a view or take one unneeded step and crucial time is lost.

The rule change put drivers and pit crews on equal footing, both needing to perform at top speed under conditions of extreme pressure. Schack described this shift in philosophical terms: "The drivers cope with that every day. So should we. When they go to qualifying, it's all about speed and all about pressure. If you take a football player who's going to take a penalty kick in a very important situation versus doing it in a practice match, it's two different things. You can do pit stop practice day in and day out, but the first pit stop in the first race is the real deal. It's very different. You'll feel a bit of the butterflies in your stomach for sure, and otherwise you're not doing the right thing. Now we're a bit more of a team—it bonds the team together. You see people high-fiving each other when they've done a good stop because it can make your position easily."

The last ingredient is the desire to win. "We always want to go down to the lowest time as the best pit stop crew in the pit lane, and that's our target. It's as simple as that. There's nothing in between the lines. We want to be the best pit stop crew." Schack continues, "Everyone looks around and says, 'Blimey, these boys have it sorted—they're on pole position every time.' If you can shave half a second off every stop compared to your competitors every time . . . half a second is a lot of time in this competitive world."

THE RIGHT NATURAL GIFTS, the right training, the ability to perform under pressure, and the overriding desire to win—these four attributes define the perfect pit crew. And the perfect team of any kind, for that matter. Ole Schack's description of Red Bull's Formula 1 racing team reflects what any high-performing organization needs to achieve. Shared experiences forge bonds within individual teams and competition between the four "corner" teams ensures that no one gets too comfortable, resulting in everyone regressing to a faster and more competitive mean.

Cultures built on speed have these traits. They give rise to teams that not only accept the need for speed—speed in decision making, alignment, and execution—but thrive on it, requiring it for their own job satisfaction. Speed cultures always start from the top, but this shared idea is mirrored by everyone, and those who aren't wired for it tend to self-select and leave for cultures more attuned to their own needs. There is simply an acknowledgment: This is how we do things here. We're fast on purpose.

For speed cultures, all things being equal, faster is better. This does not imply that corners are cut; as a matter of fact, speed cultures are often more rigorous than their alternatives precisely because they have found processes that eliminate or discourage time-wasting detours. They simply make decisions based on clearly defined criteria and encourage everyone to come prepared. Once everyone has had their say and presented their case, decisions are made and everyone commits to alignment and best efforts moving forward, regardless of the heartfelt opinions they held walking into the room. There's no time or sympathy for second guessing. Make a decision and let's execute to the best of our abilities toward that goal. This is a cultural shift for many, because often such conversions happen privately. We come around to new ways of doing things in our own time. In speed cultures, we're asked to put this tendency aside and row with the rest of the team.

This is living within a speed culture.

Speed of Decision Making: Intuit

On my team, we'd end the debate by having users vote on features or bring the users in and consider them an extension of the team. We tell users that we have a limited amount of time and dollars, so you tell us where we should focus our efforts.

—SCOTT WILDER, FORMER GENERAL MANAGER OF
ONLINE COMMUNITIES, INTUIT

Intuit lives within an industry landscape dominated by giants, so it isn't necessarily the sort of company that you'd think would be independent at this point. But it is, and it's thriving. As a matter of fact, Intuit's personal and small business financial software products like Quicken and TurboTax have become industry standards. When you ask any Silicon Valley industry watcher, they tell you the same thing: Intuit does things differently; they're a model for best practices. And more than doing things right, they do them fast.

"My first day at work, I met (Intuit founder) Scott Cook. By accident. It was clear that my experience meant nothing to him. He wanted to know my primary research—how do I know something is good." I first spoke to Scott Wilder, Intuit's former General Manager of Online Communities, just as he was preparing a presentation on how Intuit managed capturing the voice of the customer, and we quickly found ourselves on the subject of speed as a weapon. Scott described Intuit's culture as a "Learn—Teach—Learn" environment, beginning with Cook's passion for customer insight and feedback. "The whole idea of just being open and learning is key at Intuit," Wilder told me. "When Scott started the company, he launched a program called Follow Me Home. He was asking anybody and everybody from the company to wait outside a retail store until somebody bought one of our products and ask them if we could watch them use our product in their own environment. So this could be anybody using TurboTax in their home or using Quicken in their home or home office. This is pretty radical if you think about it. So that's kind of the mind-set of everybody in the company."

Intuit has built a leading suite of personal and small business financial management tools in a market segment that an outsider might assume would be ceded to a Microsoft. "Intuit has managed to not only hold off Microsoft Money but push it into a nonexistent market share, and they've done this by reducing the time from internal ideas to testing them with customers," Dr. Christopher Meyer, author of *Fast Cycle Time* and professor at the California Institute of Technology, told me. "Rather than having marketing experts who are internal to the company say what's right or what's wrong, they get them very quickly to 'pre-betas'—just workable, functional things—that you can end the internal debate on quickly."

This focus on ending the internal debate with an evidence-based decision-making culture makes Intuit an excellent study in speed. And note that Intuit is a $3 billion company with more than eight thousand employees, not a ten-person start-up.

Intuit's social communities of users interacting with the company grew out of a need to manage the increasing volume of information. "I created this online community back in 2003 . . . it was kind of a hare-brained idea," Wilder told me. "I was running the e-commerce business and I created the community Web site because I couldn't keep up with all the information our users wanted. I just did it and then presented it to the executive committee. They said it was great and to just go for it." This need to give its customers the information they needed set Intuit's first steps at community engagement in motion. But it soon became clear that the community could serve other purposes, in particular delivering on its founder's vision of decision making driven by customer insights.

"Users are making suggestions and voting and commenting on other users' product suggestions," Wilder explained. This real-time customer feedback not only helps collect feedback on ideas the Intuit team has generated, but it has also become a fertile source of new product ideas. "One of the things I look at a lot is where users are in their adoption curve of the technology," Wilder told me. "For example, most of our users were late to the blogging world. They were small business owners in middle America and blogging wasn't for them." Clearly, Intuit views all customers—not just "fans" or "monster users" or even the most vocal ones—as critical pieces of the information puzzle. As soon as someone interacts with your products, their story becomes relevant.

Intuit's culture of customer insight and continuous feedback has a clear benefit beyond new product development: They are able to quickly resolve internal debates, the kind that often impede forward progress.

"You can have someone conceptualize an idea and be very into it," Dr. Chris Meyer explained, "but until you get it into a customer's hands, someone who's not as passionate about the idea or intimate with what the intent was, you can't really tell whether the idea was worth it or not." Intuit's culture of collecting real-time feedback on new ideas, plus their ability to tap a community of users willing to share their own new product ideas gives the company's decision makers the tools they need to make evidence-based decisions instead of relying on hunches and unsupported opinion. Further, users can become decision makers. "We'd end the debate by having users vote on features, or we'd bring the users in and consider them an extension of the team," Wilder told me. "We tell users that we have a limited amount of time and dollars, so you tell us where we should focus our efforts. Then, we tell them this is what we heard and this is what we implemented." The loop is now closed and everyone feels included, heard, and ultimately happy that they are a part of the process.

Intuit is an example of a strong founder-driven culture of constant learning and fact-based decision making. This skill set and focus becomes more important as the software world changes from a distributed model of customers walking out of stores with boxes containing the latest version to a Web-based one where the software is in constant development. Now, features that affect all users simultaneously, for better or worse, can be added immediately. The more fully a brand can understand the needs of their customers, the better their products and experiences will be.

What can we learn from Intuit, and how can its lessons be applied in environments where speed isn't already part of the culture?

- **EVIDENCE BEATS OPINION.** Today, it's become incredibly easy for any company to collect customer feedback, and there's no good reason not to. A culture of curiosity can be implemented in a single team or company-wide. And having the hard evidence to quickly end internal debate means less posturing, less pontificating, and more goal-line orientation. Evidence-based decision making speeds things up.

- **QUALITATIVE FEEDBACK AND QUANTITATIVE DATA BOTH MATTER.** The pendulum tends to swing from one to the other in many companies, with one falling into and then out of favor, but let's be blunt: Both matter a lot. "One big lesson is not just to look at the numbers but also to listen carefully to what people are saying," Scott told me. "How I describe a problem isn't the same as how you'd describe a problem, and the nuance is important. The numbers are important for senior management, but when you talk to Scott Cook he wants to know what people are saying."

- **EACH ACT AN END USER MAKES FURTHER SOLIDIFIES HIS OR HER CONNECTION WITH THE BRAND.** We all feel intense personal pressure to act in a manner consistent with our previously made public statements and acts. Once a user makes a suggestion—or even comments on another's suggestion—that user changes from a passive consumer to an active participant, and becomes even more willing to engage with the brand. The sense of ownership increases and the connection becomes deeper. Users with these types of psychological bonds are more often than not better customers over a longer period of time. The benefits to the brand are clear.

Intuit shows us an example of a company built around the idea of quickly gaining customer insights, both quantitative and qualitative, and then making decisions that reflect their understanding of the stated needs of its users. The ability to shorten the internal debate and quickly move to implementation not only speeds up the process but increases confidence and internal morale through a decision-making culture that favors objective, rather than subjective, criteria.

Speed of Evolution: Direct Hit and Xfire

For the first year, we were launching an updated version of Xfire every two weeks. By the time they had their internal staff meetings, you'd already moved someplace else.

—MIKE CASSIDY, FORMER CEO OF DIRECT HIT AND XFIRE

Any discussion of speed as a competitive weapon would be incomplete without at least one story that sits squarely in the start-up space, so here are two from the same founder. Mike Cassidy is a serial entrepreneur and Silicon Valley start-up veteran known for launching fast companies: fast meaning fast to ramp up, fast to get out of the starting block, fast to get early market traction, and—critical in the Silicon Valley culture—fast to successfully exit and be acquired.

Direct Hit was a search engine built on the idea that sites with higher click volume and where visitors spent more time browsing should be rewarded with higher search rankings. Cassidy's company was funded in April 1998 by venture capital firm Draper Fisher Jurvetson, and as with everything else, it happened quickly. "Direct Hit was a playbook on how fast you could move," Cassidy told me. "We pitched Draper Jurvetson at 8:50 in the morning and we got a term sheet the same day before I even got on the plane to go home. Eleven days later we opened the office. We'd rented a space, we'd gotten computers and a phone system."

The pace picked up from there. Within a month, Direct Hit landed its first deal with Hotbot, one of the top five largest search engines of 1998. "We hadn't even built the product yet," Cassidy explained. "It was only one month into the company. We told them if we built it, it would do this and that, and they said, 'OK, we'll do a deal with you.' We launched in August with Hotbot, and it worked so well that after a few months of working with Hotbot we did a deal with AOL and also with Apple." Eight months later, Direct Hit had its search results on MSN Search and Lycos, securing the rest of the major search engines. Six months after that, at the end of 1998, Direct Hit was acquired for $530 million by the search engine Ask Jeeves. "That was very fast-paced," Cassidy said. "We had to get deals with these search engines very quickly and build the product very quickly. Three months after we opened the doors, the product was ready." A $530 million exit after a little less than two years.

Cassidy's second major venture was an instant messaging platform for gamers called Xfire. While the company would launch with specific functionality for gamers, the competitive landscape was filled with massive players like AIM (AOL Instant Messenger), Yahoo! Messenger, and MSN Messenger. The company's first start, however, was a hiccup—one quickly rectified with Cassidy's typical emphasis on speed and execution. The company's original incarnation, Ultimate Arena, was a site that offered cash rewards to gamers who won online tournaments. Cassidy soon realized this wasn't quite the sweet spot, and retooled; three months later, he launched Xfire.

"Our strategy was to launch quickly and get feedback from users as to what features they liked, didn't like, and thought worked very well," Cassidy told me. "For the first year, we were launching an updated version of Xfire every two weeks. That makes it very difficult for a competitor to keep pace, because even if they decide, 'Wow that's a product we have to reckon with,' for most larger companies it takes them quite a while to put together an analysis of how to compete and have meetings and design a competitive product. If we're putting out a new product every two weeks, we have ten or twenty new versions of the product out in that same time period." By MTV's acquisition of Xfire in the spring of 2004, for $110 million, the company had 16 million customers using its software an average of eighty-eight hours per month.

What is it about Cassidy's management philosophy that makes things happen so fast? He identified three things that matter to him. The first is rapid alignment. "The very first day when the company forms and we sit down together, I tell people, here's my philosophy: Whenever we have a meeting to debate something I want everyone to scream and say, 'Mike, that's the stupidest thing I've ever heard and here's why.' You have to have data and facts but be totally frank and direct about why something's stupid. But at the end of the meeting when we've made a decision, I want everyone to come together and say, 'Fifteen minutes ago I hated it, but now I see a way to make it better,' and never look back and say 'I told you so.' You can never have that and have a high-performance team." Encourage robust debate, even among fairly abrasive personalities, but when the decision is made, everyone must come into alignment and move in unison toward the chosen goal.

Second, Cassidy emphasized the importance of what he described as "20X developers." "Truly outstanding people are more than 20 percent better than the next guy," he explained. "We talk about 20X developers—people who do in one day what a good developer takes twenty days to do, and I really believe that. A total of three people built the Xfire instant messenger product that went on to have 16 million users and was worth $110 million, and a total of three engineers built the Direct Hit search engine that grew to a market value of $530 million. Look for those extraordinary partners who are worth far more than the ordinary person."

Last, Cassidy described drive. "Small companies are more often defeated by internal friction than by external competitors," he explained. "Human nature creates friction between people, especially when you're in a pressure cooker situation. The first mover advantage might get five million users and the next person might get nothing. You're looking for that person who wants to be first out, and that person might cause more friction than the next guy who's more easygoing."

To Mike Cassidy, speed is a function of culture, of hiring top performers who may clash but are able to quickly align, and who all recognize the importance of speed as a competitive advantage.

Not everyone works for a small, nimble start-up, but anyone can take enduring lessons away from Cassidy's experience. What can we learn from Direct Hit and Xfire?

- **DESIGN PROCESSES FOR SPEED.** Direct Hit landed its first deal before its product was even built. This is usually frowned upon in large organizations with clearly delineated processes for new product development. But squint and understand the underlying value of the lesson. What can you remove? What can you pull forward? Can you combine steps or eliminate bottlenecks by questioning the givens in a defined process? Can you build contingencies in your sales process that allow you to move faster than your engineering and manufacturing would normally allow? Decide what the real bottlenecks should be, not what they are, and go from there.

- **MANAGE WITH MOMENTUM.** Open debate and an environment that provides people the opportunity (and safety) to speak their minds is crucial—and fairly uncommon. Approach this with caution. But if you are willing to embrace this idea fully and give your team the ability to flesh out their ideas and then defend them passionately and without fear of repercussions, you will have taken the first step. The second critical component is coming to rapid closure on a chosen course of action and securing your team's commitment that, once a decision is made, they will all throw themselves into its successful implementation without reservation. It's a two-way street, and high-functioning teams cannot embark on this path halfheartedly. We all have egos, and the insidious impulse to say "I told you so" needs to be repressed.

- **HIGH PERFORMERS AREN'T ALWAYS THE EASIEST TO GET ALONG WITH.** Managing stars is a tricky business. There are schools of thought that say they should be given the benefit of the doubt and a bit more freedom than others, and there are others that tell us that "the graveyards are filled with indispensable men." Both approaches can work, so you have to decide where on this spectrum you fall.

While they capture the best of working in a start-up environment, the lessons of Mike Cassidy's successes can be applied broadly to any fast-moving work environment where time to market and to critical mass are central.

Speed of Execution: WellDyne

It's not about hustle and working faster. We don't allow silos to exist. Having come from a company with thirty thousand employees with silos everywhere, I'm very familiar with what silos look like and the problems they cause.

—DAMIEN LAMENDOLA, CEO OF WELLDYNE

When I first mentioned the title of my book to Damien Lamendola, the CEO of WellDyne, he laughed. When you've spent more than twenty years working for giants and dealing with fast-moving upstarts running between your feet and causing mayhem, you gain a healthy respect for any competitor who can do what your employer can't. But now, the idea of toppling a giant or two suits him just fine.

Lamendola bought the prescription benefits management business of Dura Pharmaceuticals in 2003, and since then this former "nonstrategic asset" has, in Lamendola's words, "been growing like crazy." The company's core business, prescription benefit management, handles the drug plans for the employees of corporate health care programs. When you're on an insurance plan with an employer and you go into a drugstore to get a prescription filled, it's a company like Lamendola's that handles the calculation of your co-pay, the billing to the employer or the managed care organization, the process that verifies you haven't filled your prescription elsewhere, and the payments to the drug companies. And while this may sound like a backroom business without a lot of competition, it isn't. With the health care industry growing by leaps and bounds, not to mention a rapidly aging demographic in the United States, WellDyne is locked in competition with a host of larger, publicly traded companies. But while he doesn't have as much market heft as these well-financed competitors, he makes it up in speed.

Lamendola's game plan for creating a culture of speed within a mature and highly competitive part of the health care industry rests on three pillars. The first is eliminating the internal organizational boundaries—the "silos"—that so often define larger corporations. Removing these artificial fiefdoms means information moves faster—and with faster information comes faster decision making. By breaking down the barriers within the corporate structure, accountability is more transparent, information flows more freely, and managers with a propensity to get involved with operational details get to the heart of the matter that much faster. "We have over two hundred employees and no administrative assistants," he explained. "When we set up our operations in Florida, for example, we didn't put a general manager down there. Our vice president of operations manages both locations as if they were one. We have a lean organization that doesn't allow for silos to exist."

The second major point of departure is how the company has organized its systems. "We're faster and more nimble in our ability to set up the systems and customize their plan the way they want it set up," Lamendola explained. "You may be a hospital with three thousand employees and you have a hospital pharmacy. We can set up a system that is unique to you. We're a lean and mean and quick-moving operation. One of our wholesale drug suppliers called us and said they had a client that just bought a pharmacy operation and they need help selling the prescription drugs. We called the client the same day, sent them a nondisclosure agreement, and had a joint venture operating the next week. The big guys can't do this. It takes them a month to set up a meeting. It all has to do with speed."

Any company that can evaluate an opportunity on Monday and have a working joint venture operating by the end of the next week is built for speed. What makes an organization move that fast is leadership, and it is Lamendola's leadership philosophy that resides at the heart of the enterprise.

"I move back and forth between the daily operations up to the strategic level across the entire operation," he explained. "That's probably the number one factor in making us fast. I see a lot of companies where the CEO is detached and not involved with the day-to-day operations. I'm involved. We're a two hundred million dollar operation. When we started up the operation in Florida, my CFO and I were the selection committee. We worked with the state economic development agency. In order to have that kind of speed, you have to have a CEO in place with that kind of culture and step in at that level."

But how scalable is this sort of approach? Can a CEO be deeply involved in both operational and strategic decision as a company grows? How far can anyone stretch? "We could easily grow to be a five billion dollar company."

WellDyne gives us an excellent example of a business-to-business service-based company that competes on the basis of institutionalized speed: speed of structure, systems, and culture. What lessons can you take away from WellDyne?

- **COMPANIES THAT HAVE TROUBLE COMMUNICATING DON'T NEED TO COMMUNICATE MORE—THEY NEED TO REDUCE THE NEED TO COMMUNICATE.** Organizing for speed is more about eliminating information bottlenecks than anything else. WellDyne doesn't allow silos to exist—and silos create artificial barriers between people and decisions.

- **SPEED IS A CULTURAL CHOICE, REGARDLESS OF SCOPE.** This works within a team just as easily as it does at a departmental, divisional, or corporate level. "You can be as involved in any department as I am with this company," Lamendola explained. "Walk around and have a feel for what's going on. Don't simply rely on chain of command. Be involved with the tactical stuff and also step up and do the strategy. Anyone can accelerate the speed and the success of the organization if they do that."

- **RAPID ALIGNMENT DRIVES EXECUTION.** This still means that everyone's voice can be heard, but, as in Mike Cassidy's case, alignment means that once a decision is made, the team moves forward together toward the best possible implementation.

There's nothing about WellDyne's industry space or customer base that dictates a culture of speed. This desire to be faster and more nimble than its larger competitors comes from within. It's a cultural decision, first and foremost, but it also manifests itself in structure and systems. WellDyne shows us an example of winning on the basis of speed where speed isn't necessarily an indigenous characteristic of the industry—and this should be inspiring to all of us.

Speed of Mobilization:
Scott Brown, R-MA

We consistently felt like we were the underdog. We were. We were going to be out-staffed. They probably had more people on their communications campaign than we had on our entire campaign staff.

—ROB WILLINGTON, SOCIAL MEDIA STRATEGIST FOR SCOTT BROWN'S U.S. SENATE CAMPAIGN

It took four and a half months, starting with a discussion sitting around a table on whether to run in the special election to the night of his acceptance speech, for Scott Brown to overturn the forty-seven-year Democratic stranglehold of one Massachusetts Senate seat. What was referred to in the contentious campaign as "Ted Kennedy's seat" was handed over to a charismatic, libertarian-leaning politician relatively unknown outside his home state, sending a jolt throughout the U.S. political landscape. Regardless of your political leanings, Scott Brown's successful Senate campaign holds a number of valuable lessons in applying speed as a competitive weapon.

Rob Willington, now a principal at Swiftcurrent Strategies,

was Brown's Web and political strategist on the campaign. "It all started in late August [2009], when we first sat around the table talking about running," he explained to me. "We didn't have much money and we didn't have a lot of institutional support because the entire state is Democrat. We couldn't call a local congressman and say hey, we need your network. Our networks had to be built from the ground up. To make things worse, it was a special election. We only had four and a half months."

The campaign was an uphill fight against not only an overwhelmingly larger political machine but a general population that hadn't elected a Republican in most of their lifetimes. Willington decided to focus the team's efforts online to make the most of its limited campaign funds. As with many political campaigns, the opening drive is important. Fortunately, Brown had already heeded Willington's advice before the decision to run was even a pipe dream.

"When I was working with the state party in 2005," Willington said, "I wrote a memo to all the Republican legislators on Beacon Hill about Facebook and why you'd want an account and how you'd apply it in the political world." The memo emphasized "the importance of not just talking about politics but about family vacations and pumpkin carving with your kids. Also reaching out and connecting with people outside your district in case you ever want to run for a larger office or statewide, so you'd have people around the state who are familiar with you and can be the initiators around whom you can build the local and regional efforts of your campaign. Out of all of them, Scott was the only one who took that memo and started a Facebook campaign." When Brown approached Willington about helping him with the Senate race, his Facebook page had been up for a couple of years, with three or four thousand people around the state already connected. "Granted, it wasn't huge," Willington said, "but it was valuable in the sense that people already knew who he was. It was up and running for maybe two years."

Starting a political campaign with several thousand hand-raisers created a halo effect. "Because he was the only Republican that initially took that stance [on Facebook], he became the Republican voice for all GOP activists across the state who were on Facebook." Brown's early jump into social media gave his campaign credibility online; his presence there looked natural and authentic, not like a campaign tactic.

With an active and growing social media hub as an anchor, the campaign then seized the opportunity to present its message early and often: "We focused early on building the persona, the personality, the character of who Scott is. We did this with a heavy use of video. It was inexpensive—free, actually. It was an easy way to pump out content." With relatively cheap Mac-based editing tools, video was quickly produced and put online. "When we advertised our new Web videos, we'd put it up on YouTube, but we would use the embed code and use it on our donation page. That way, when we advertised it we'd send people to the donation page."

As the campaign picked up momentum, with a thriving on-line presence and a growing war chest, the focus moved off-line. "We wanted to blow it up online so we could then take it off-line—boots on the ground, door knocking and phone banking... a very massive get-out-the-vote operation. We believed we had enough voters in Massachusetts to vote for Scott Brown, so it wasn't so much about motivation as mobilization."

By using instant messaging tools geared toward getting the candidate's hand-raisers to call in to talk radio shows, the campaign successfully melded the newest of technologies with the oldest. "We used text messaging because people wouldn't even need to dial a number," Willington told me. "You could be sitting in your car and all of a sudden become an activist for Scott Brown." The results were a boon to the campaign, with Brown supporters representing the vocal majority of supportive calls to Brown during his radio appearances. These same callers were also calling in whenever Brown's opponent, Martha Coakley, appeared. As any PR manager—or political candidate—would agree, you can't prepare for every question, so when a well-organized group of thousands start asking the questions most relevant to each of them individually, Coakley ran out of talking points, concluding one uncomfortable radio interview in an exasperated tone, "I'm really happy that all the Republicans are up and listening this morning because every call that has come in has been a Scott Brown call." "This was a great way to get people to take ownership, like a low dollar donor," Willington explained. "Once they do this, they're in the game now. They're an investor. The quality of the questions was so good they gave us Web video content."

Once someone has pushed "send," the die is cast. They've just taken an irreversible step, psychologically committing themselves to being more than just a passive supporter. "We're getting a lot of people to contribute a little bit," Willington explained. "We had this model from our call from home program, where the average person made twelve or thirteen calls from home. The same thing from the text messaging, the same thing from online donations. Our average online donation was $80, and we raised over $12.5 million a month. That's a lot of people contributing a lot of money."

On the evening of January 19, 2010, Scott Brown was declared the special election winner with a 53 percent to 46 percent margin of victory. "We consistently felt like we were the underdog. We were. We were going to be outmanned, outstaffed. They probably had more people on their communications campaign than we had on our entire campaign staff. Knowing that, we had to operate that much more efficiently, even internally in how we used cloud computing to collaborate so we didn't have multiple versions of a budget or a press release or voter goals and plans; we were just working off one version. And so one of the reasons we were able to move so quickly on so many initiatives is that we were so small. Big campaigns have a tendency to get bogged down in a committee mentality."

What enduring lessons from the Scott Brown campaign can we apply broadly—not just to political campaigns but to brands?

- **YOUR PLATFORM IS THE BASE OF SUPPORT FOR YOUR CAMPAIGN AND YOUR BRAND.** Building up a list of "hand-raisers"—people who are ready and willing to hear what you have to say—is critical in launching a campaign. The sooner you get this started and the more seriously you take this small step, the faster you can start. Scott Brown made the decision to run in the special election four and a half months before the event, but he began with three to four thousand Facebook fans.

- **SOCIAL MEDIA IS ABOUT SPEED OF ACTIVATION.** If you have direct, one-to-one contact with a group of volunteers, the time it takes to get your message out—in an age of hand-held computing and instant messaging—is measured in seconds.

- **UNDERSTAND THE PROCESS OF COMMITMENT AND EVANGELISM.** We all feel tremendous psychological pressure to behave in a manner consistent with actions and statements we've willingly and publicly made; once someone has taken action and made a donation or a phone call or even called in to a radio station to ask a question, they're no longer on the sidelines. They're your frontline activists.

- **USE THE RIGHT TECHNOLOGY AT THE RIGHT TIME TO DO THE RIGHT THINGS.** The campaign made sophisticated use of Web-based instant messaging to activate its members via their mobile phones in an effort to drive them to call in to talk radio.

The Scott Brown U.S. Senate campaign gives us a vivid example of a "brand launch"—that happens to be a political campaign—enabled and accelerated by the smart use of social media. From Facebook to YouTube to Twitter to instant messaging, the use of technology and social tools amplified and accelerated the efforts of those volunteers on the street and on the phones. In this case, we see that the real benefit of social media isn't so much being an end in and of itself, but as a means—the means to activate, motivate, and amplify behaviors.

Key Takeaways

Speed discusses how smart brands can create cultures of speed and move faster than the giants they face. From cultures to processes to the use of technology, each example highlights how brands, people, and ideas can move so fast that the giant can't catch them. What key takeaways can we extract from these examples that anyone could apply?

Decision making is a cultural phenomenon. The speed at which you are able to get past the posturing phase, where egos run free and evidence is seldom seen, is a predictor of success. We've all been in that meeting and in that company. Someone with more title than evidence has an opinion that must be shared. This is how things slow down. Our job is to acknowledge this block quickly and put steps in place through group behavior—rules, rituals—to ensure it doesn't become a habit. Establishing a culture where posturing without evidence is quickly quashed is a good first step.

In the Internet age, there is no reason not to collect data, both qualitative and quantitative. How much data is spilling out into the ether every day in your company? How many different data traps can you set up that give you the excuse you need to foster a meaningful dialogue? What would this degree of customer insight do for your decision making? Our role here is to let nothing go to waste and to actively seek out those areas where data is being collected but not analyzed, as well as determine where small changes to procedures could in turn gather critically important data that would otherwise be lost.

Gather information quickly and move to rapid execution. While this is a cultural point, it is also rooted deeply in your own personal leadership skills. Set these expectations early and manage your team's activities toward this important end. Agree up front what you expect: evidence-based insights, recommendations, vigorous debate, alignment, closure, and then ruthless execution. There's no room on high-performing teams for "I told you so" behavior or harboring ill feelings for a course of action because of a difference of opinion. We all need to be on the same page from the start and agree that this is how we will act from here on out. You can do this on a team level or a company level. Be fast on purpose.

Fostering a culture of meaningful customer contact turns supporters into activists. Once a user submits a suggestion and receives feedback and acknowledgment for it, that user has irrevocably changed. They are no longer passive supporters—they have become activists. Once a registered voter pushes "send" on their cell phone and confronts a rival candidate, live on the phone, that person is no longer on the fence. They are committed to the cause.

The psychology says that when we take voluntary, public stances on a position, we feel significant social pressure—both internally as well as externally—to behave in a consistent manner. Once we take a stand, we become more radicalized in our beliefs. An end user having meaningful contact with Intuit about Quicken is no longer ambivalent about which personal finance product they'd recommend—they're committed. This means the more we engage our customers, question them, and then recognize and apply what we've heard from them, the more loyal they become. This is a very virtuous circle.

Surround yourself with similarly focused people. This is a cultural hiring decision. Find those "20X developers" and others who want to be the first ones to the finish line. Goal line orientation is the most coveted trait I know of in a new hire. I used to call them "handlers"—those treasured employees you could turn to in a hurry and say, "handle it!" and you'd know, walking away, that the job would be handled professionally, correctly, and on time.

If structural silos are slowing down decision making, remove them if you can. If you can't, find ways to make them irrelevant. We can't casually change the organizational structure of our companies for a host of very good reasons, but we can change how we, personally, get things done within them. Our job is to establish informal relationships so that we can foster a climate of real-time collaboration, instant communication, and approval. Kill bureaucracy wherever you see it and find workarounds when you can't. Anyone can do this, regardless of pay grade or title.

Understand the power of a platform. How many of your customers can you identify by name? How many would drop everything and do something for you right now? Unless you've paid significant attention to this already, the number probably is fairly small. The faster you can build a trust-based, personal, connected network with people who have self-identified as being willing to help you, the better. It doesn't matter whether you're a politician or a marketing manager. It will help you immeasurably no matter what you do, and all it takes is time, effort, and a willingness to share something of yourself. You may not think you need this today, but you can't wait until you do to try to develop it. Start now.

Understand your technological options. Scott Brown would have been a very long shot indeed if he hadn't been able to jumpstart his campaign with several thousand Facebook friends or activate his core through instant messaging. The convergence of computing and telephony, of content creation and consumption and the blurring of lines between information and entertainment are all powerful changes that you, as a businessperson, can leverage. Know what's available, talk to your peers and network, and execute scalable tests so you can ramp up quickly when your time comes.

You can create a culture of speed—whether of decision making, of execution, or of customer activation—regardless of where you are in the organization.

CHAPTER THREE: *Winning in the Last Three Feet*

In every transaction, there's a moment just after the giant thinks he's got the sale and just before the customer hands over their money. This gap is an opportunity for a smart, agile competitor to snatch victory from the jaws of defeat.

Winning in the Last Three Feet is an old retail expression, but it speaks universally to the idea of understanding that it's never over until it's over. You can have a brilliant campaign—or a brilliant product—but you can't assume the rest will take care of itself. It never does.

Those last three feet are where giant-killers live.

It started in the twelfth when Conn rocked Louis. Now he goes back to his corner and he says, "I'm going to knock this guy out." His corner man says, "What are you crazy? You've got the fight won." But Conn goes out to knock him out and has the best of it until Louis catches him with the upper cut and knocks him down. He's counted out at two minutes and fifty-eight seconds in the thirteenth round.

—BERT SUGAR, BOXING HISTORIAN, WRITER, AND INDUCTEE
TO THE INTERNATIONAL BOXING HALL OF FAME

In June 1941, boxing legend Joe Louis was facing a shocking upset at the hands of former light heavyweight champion Billy Conn at the Polo Grounds in New York, in what has been described by many as the greatest fight in boxing history. Louis was at the height of his fame, power, and abilities. His right cross started somewhere deep within the earth under his right foot and shot upward in a compact, smooth transfer of body weight that had once put "Two-Ton" Tony Galento on his back for the one and only time in his career. But on this night, Conn—with matinee idol looks, fighting at what today seems like an impossibly light 169 pounds—was simply too smart and too fast. After twelve rounds, he was ready to finish the champion off.

"I saw it on radio," the iconic boxing historian and raconteur Bert Sugar told me. "It started in the twelfth round. Conn rocked Louis. You can see his foot come off the canvas and he grabbed Conn. And at that point, Conn—who was not really a knockout puncher—goes back to his corner and says, 'I'm going to knock this guy out.' His corner man, Johnny Ray Pitler, says, 'You're crazy—you've got the fight won.' But Conn says he's going to knock him out."

As one contemporary reporter described it, Conn "came down off his toes" after staggering Louis in the preceding rounds and slugged it out with the champion until 2:58 of the fight's thirteenth and final round, when Louis connected with a short right upper cut that traveled about a foot. Conn dropped to the canvas like a felled tree and was counted out. "Afterward," Sugar told me, "Jesse Abrams goes into the locker room and asks him, 'Billy, what happened out there?' And Conn, always the imp, says, 'What's the sense of being Irish if you can't be dumb?' "

Once Conn realized that he had the chance to win the world heavyweight title by knockout, he was no longer interested in winning by unanimous decision alone. He wanted to knock the great Joe Louis out. Louis knew that he was losing, too. He knew he needed a knockout to win. Conn graciously stood still long enough to oblige him.

Boxing is unlike most other sports. In boxing, you can win with one punch. In baseball, tennis, track, football, and most other sports, you must come from behind, catch up, and then pass your opponent. In boxing, you can fight a perfect fight and lose in the final second. Or, in the case of Joe Louis, take a beating and then win it all with one punch.

The process, the road that got you there, all the celebrity and interviews and praise that surround you are beside the point. What matters is the final, ultimate result of all the preparation and work.

What matters is finishing.

GIANTS HAVE MORE RESOURCES—money and people, usually—than you do, and they will throw these at problems and opportunities alike. Said another way, they're very good at starting things. They can create significant awareness through their efforts, from foot traffic in retail stores to search traffic online, because they're willing and able to spend the money needed to make it happen. Giants are excellent at doing the heavy lifting, like paying for splashy advertising campaigns, street teams, sports sponsorships, and "buzz-worthy" events. Giants are giants because they have the market heft to get the attention of lots and lots of people.

There's a flip side to this. They may have more money and people than you do, but they also have the bureaucracy that you don't. They have mandatory meetings, layers of management, and, most important, deeply instilled corporate cultures. In fairness, the giant's culture may be its greatest strength—but it may also be your greatest blessing, because while your counterpart may have more resources to work with than you do, your counterpart also goes home every night with his or her own dreams and aspirations, one of which may be to succeed in his or her career within that same giant. You get ahead in a giant by working within their culture. You get very good at staff meetings, project management flow processes, playing by the rules.

Your counterpart has to become a master of bureaucracy. It is likely, therefore, that you have the opportunity to take advantage of their distraction and win with a clearly focused strike when the giant thinks it's done its job and has moved on to the next item on its ponderous to-do list.

This is a perfect situation for the giant-killer, because you don't want to have to spend the kind of money needed to drive all this demand. You just want to spend enough to switch the customer when they're ready to spend. So let the giant pay for getting your customers off the couch, through the parking lot, and ready to buy. When they're standing in the aisle with their wallet in hand, they are the most qualified they will ever be.

Winning in the Last Three Feet reminds us never to assume your potential customer has already made up their mind. Yes, they may have researched your giant's product for months. Yes, they may have strong preference for your giant's brand, too. But you've got a face-to-face opportunity where they have marketing. You've got social and they've got messaging. Even when you're working in a virtual space, you've got the opportunity to spark interest in the buyer's mind because you've just injected a sense of competition into the game. Everyone wants validation, and few are so sure in their knowledge that they'll ignore the advice of an "expert" standing in front of them, even when that expert isn't terribly credentialed. In a culture rife with invidious comparison, where the definition of an ignoramus is someone who doesn't know what you learned five minutes ago, we love to get the slightly newer, the incrementally more exclusive, or the esoteric choice preferred by those in the know that your friends haven't heard of. Yet.

There are many opportunities to take advantage of a rising

tide, from seasonality to giant-initiated marketing events. You just have to be there when it happens, ready to do business. Can you catch the attention of half your giant's customers? A quarter? If you can take 10 percent away at the point of influence, you've done your job.

You don't have to win everywhere. Concentrate on winning at the point of influence. Concentrate on finishing well.

Close and strike. Time to win in the last three feet.

Winning at the Point of Purchase: Adobe

I remember the day the buyer notified me that we'd lost the spot to Microsoft. I remember exactly where I was in that moment in time. I was shocked.

—MANDY TORVICK, CHANNEL MANAGER FOR RETAIL SALES, ADOBE

Adobe, the company that makes software many of us use to view and manage images and documents on our computers, was selling a consumer photo editing suite called Photoshop Elements. Microsoft's Microsoft Digital Image Pro was the competitive product, positioned aggressively against the Adobe product and undercutting Photoshop Element's street price at retail.

Adobe's largest big box retailer had promised them the category's only advertising space for the "Black Friday" holiday weekend in 2003, referring to the day after Thanksgiving that marks the beginning of the holiday selling season for most retailers. This is one of the top three weekend selling periods of the year for most retailers, and consequently it isn't volume that can easily be replaced if the event is missed. Promises were made, volume commitments given to management, and expectations set. Then, the rug was pulled out from beneath the carefully laid plan, putting the sales forecast—and Mandy Torvick, Adobe's channel manager for retail sales—in a bind. The call came in telling her that her ad placement would be given to rival Microsoft instead.

"After I got over my anger, I viewed it as an opportunity to be a leader," Torvick explained. Instead of reloading and waiting for their next shot at an ad with the retailer, she planned a guerilla campaign to hit interested consumers when they were in the stores, ads in hand, and ready to buy. Analyzing sell-through, she picked the top 50 percent of stores by unit volume—roughly 260 stores out of the chain's then total of 600—and sent retail demonstrators, hired and trained to present the product to consumers face-to-face, into each targeted store to do live demonstrations of the product.

Aaron Duran, the account manager at the time from the retail demo agency ChannelForce, described the program simply: "We knocked it out of the park . . . The ROI was much greater than anything we could have gotten on the ad given the cost of the ad and the expected sell-through."

A Black Friday ad placement would not only drive incremental foot traffic to the stores but would secure a commitment by the retailer to buy more inventory to support the event—often as much as 200 to 300 percent of what normally would be sold during this period. The cost to the manufacturer to secure the ad in question was approximately $80,000. Adobe's decision to run retail demonstrations on top of Microsoft's ad took advantage of this flood of qualified foot traffic and countered with something even more psychologically sticky than a discount on a flyer: a live person, presenting a similar product, face-to-face. Forget the fact that we all find it somewhat harder to disappoint another person and pick someone else's product. When confronted with an "authority"—regardless of the strength of his or her credentials—we all tend to take their advice, all things being equal. It's how we're wired.

Adobe's guerilla campaign didn't get them the same level of inventory buy-in that they might have expected with an ad, but their actions did drive significant incremental sell-through volume to the point where virtually all of the selected stores sold out by the end of the weekend. Notably, Adobe didn't have to deeply discount their products for the in-store effort, protecting the brand with a higher perceived value. Last, their guerilla campaign took volume away from what Microsoft would have expected to see from their investment. In short, they played the hand they were dealt with remarkable skill and averted a potential disaster.

What enduring lessons can we take away from Adobe?

- **IT'S ALL ABOUT FINISHING WELL.** Understand the point-to-point mechanics of how your stuff ends up in your customers' hands. Attach yourself to an order—understand the touch points from the consumer's initial awareness of the product or category through traditional advertising, online search, or social media all the way through the in-store merchandising experience—and see what you learn about potential weak spots in your competitor's assumptions.

- **CAPITALIZE ON OPPORTUNITY.** "Whenever there's an opportunity for foot traffic, from either a season or a competitor, you really have to capitalize on it," Torvick explained. "Regardless of whether you get the ad space, you always have an opportunity in stores to promote your product and take advantage of that traffic."

- **PLAN FOR TROUBLE.** Losing a key merchandising opportunity promised by an important partner happens in life and in business, but that doesn't mean you can't make doubly sure that it won't happen today or tomorrow. And never stop working just because you've been told you got the ad.

- **BE READY WHEN TROUBLE ARRIVES.** One of the most enduring lessons that the Adobe story teaches a careful reader is that you should have the resources ready when the opportunity (or the disaster) arises. If ChannelForce hadn't been trained and ready to deploy as part of Adobe's arsenal of weapons, this couldn't have happened. They would have watched Microsoft take their ad and the subsequent volume. Having the foresight to train and retain the right resources is half the battle.

Adobe launched a very well-orchestrated campaign to take back the opportunity they thought they had lost. Instead of an $80,000 investment, the company spent a total of $12,000 and sold out of the stores where the demos were given. Since that time, Microsoft's competitive product, Digital Image Pro, has been discontinued. Adobe gives us a smart example of playing the hand you've been dealt.

Winning at the Point of Influence: Classe

We knew we had to solve this problem—there's no amount of training that would make someone comfortable with this kind of change . . . the answer was that they'd have to have it in their house to be totally comfortable with it.

—DAVID NAUBER, EVP OF MARKETING, CLASSE

Winning hearts and minds is a question of first-person experience. You can train people, but there's a limit beyond which training can't help. Mastery happens when the "work" brain is turned off and the "life" brain reengages, when we do things on purpose rather than by rote memorization. Customers know the difference between mastery and fakery. Experience matters.

If you're like David Nauber and literally have saved your lunch money since childhood to upgrade your stereo system, you know Classe, where Nauber is EVP of marketing. Classe, a leading designer and manufacturer of high-end amplifiers aimed at the custom installation market, launched in 1980. For twenty-one years, they successfully navigated dramatic changes in the consumer electronics marketplace—from analog to digital, from stereo to multichannel, from transistors to integrated circuits—a series of transitions that wiped out most companies in their space. In 2001, a new distribution agreement with loudspeaker company Bowers & Wilkins became a merger, giving the Classe team "a clean sheet of paper," as Nauber described it: the opportunity to reinvent the brand and rethink what a high-end audio company should be. This process launched what was to become the hallmark Classe touch-screen product line.

To fully understand Classe's story, let's look at a day in the life of the high-end custom electronics business. What was once occupied solely by small boutiques catering to highly involved hobbyists has grown to include the home improvement market as well. "Customers might have come into the market attracted to a high-end projection television screen and they needed an audio system that matched the caliber of the TV—sometimes audio is an add-on to the video. Sometimes people are building new houses and they're interested in putting a home theater system in the house, so they end up talking to a high-end custom electronic design and installation specialist. They may have no knowledge of the brands, but they want a nice home theater. So we're relying on our dealers to access these customers who have enough money to buy our product, sometimes without even a product demonstration, to spend up to six figures on a high-end theater system. One guy may take six months to decide on the amplifier he wants, and on the other hand you'll have a guy who has no idea what he's buying but will spend $150,000 in an afternoon. And everything in between."

In order to succeed where half your market has little to no knowledge of your brand, you need to win the hearts and minds of the salespeople who will be demonstrating your product, justifying its premium cost, and convincing customers that it's worth choosing over all the other options. They need more than training; they need to be true believers.

"Our new touch-screen product—the Delta series—was intimidating," Nauber explained. "It was easy to use, but it was new. And salespeople wouldn't sell something that might embarrass them. They have to believe they can put it into an installation and they won't get phone calls." When it comes to selling the seller on the product, Nauber continued, "You can't spend an hour and walk away and expect the sales guy gets it."

To solve the problem, Nauber had to navigate a serious constraint: how to get salespeople to not only understand but care about these products, when the systems sometimes cost more than these people could earn in a year.

"We knew we had to solve this problem—there's no amount of training that would make someone comfortable with this kind of change," Nauber told me. "But if they don't use it right away, it's all lost. The answer was that they'd have to have it in their house to be totally comfortable with it." But how could they afford it? Nauber explained: "We had to get it in their hands before they sold a single piece, and we had to make it low-risk enough so that if they never sold one they were still going to get a really good deal—they were going to have a long time to pay for it. There was no reason to say no."

In the custom installation world, the Classe For Me program is considered the channel loyalty program par excellence. Everyone wants to do something like "what Classe did," and for good reason. The program offered salespeople the opportunity to own Classe components at 50 percent off list price with no money down and the chance to pay it off at zero percent interest over two years in eight quarterly payments. If you sold a Classe product, 5 percent of the list price would be credited to your amount due. It didn't take long for salespeople to sell more than they owed.

Was it successful? "It bought us the mindshare and the confidence in the product to establish a new, reinvented brand," Nauber told me. In addition, resellers who participated had a higher correlation of increased sell-through per storefront for the two and a half years between 2006 and the end of 2008 that the program ran. Classe For Me not only won hearts and minds but drove long-term behavioral changes as well.

Nauber sums up the program's impact: "I still think of this as paying a dividend today—because we had already solved the problem a few years ago, we were able to launch the right product (the touch-screen Delta series) at the right time, and people got it immediately. We didn't have to do much training. The benefits of the program have been long lasting. We're seeing competing lines getting dropped from the stores. Our footprint has grown as a result."

What enduring lessons can we take away from Classe?

- **WIN WHERE THE OTHER GUY DOESN'T THINK TO COMPETE.** Quick—how many other ways could Classe have tried to solve this problem? Traditional advertising, highly technical "speeds and feeds" PR aimed at audio aficionados, loyalty programs, cash-back spiffs, and a host of other avenues were all easy alternatives for Classe. We do these things because we're busy and we don't always have time to think through what needs to be done. The object of the game is changing behavior and removing constraints. Classe did this with a simple, elegant solution.

- **LEVERAGE THE POWER OF FIRST PERSON.** Experience is the best teacher, and only through experience can you naturally, effortlessly share what you've learned with others. The familiarity is unmistakable.

- **TRAINING AND MINDSHARE ARE NEVER CHECK-THE-BOX ACTIVITIES.** How could Classe For Me have gone wrong? How many online certification modules could they have produced that would have cost more money and taken more time, all while failing to change behavior?

- **SIMPLE IS ALMOST ALWAYS BEST.** How many different ways could Classe have structured this program? How many points programs, rebates, and other assorted spiffs have we all seen? Get it for half off, pay for it over two years, get 5 percent of what you sell off of what you owe. And you start using the stuff in your home today. That's it.

- **GET CLOSER TO THE CUSTOMER.** Tell me who the customer is again? The customer is the one making the buying decision. And in Classe's case, sometimes that's the guy in the middle, helping the architect or designer working on the new house. When half your business comes from people who never even see a demo, you need to make sure you're paying attention to the people who actually make the decision.

Classe gives us an excellent example of winning at the point of influence. The company created experts by making them owners. Where others provided training, Classe provided experience. Customers know the difference—and when you're spending $150,000 on a home theater and multizone audio installation, you pay attention to what the experts recommend. All the advertising, PR, and industry awards in the world won't unseat the recommendation of an installation expert who passionately believes in the product he owns himself.

Winning at the Point of Research: Oslo University

The competitor—we couldn't find them on search . . . so we agreed that search was the right thing even though the budget was fifty thousand krone—almost nothing!

—SANDER ALTEN, IPROSPECT NORWAY

A few short months before applications were due, Oslo University came to online marketing agency iProspect for help in arresting the declining enrollment it had seen in its management school. Their largest competitor for management higher education, the Norwegian School of Management, had three times their enrollment and was outspending them two hundred to one in marketing, running television, radio, and outdoor ads. Meanwhile, Oslo University had a budget of 50,000 Norwegian krone, or roughly $8,500, to spend on the effort.

However, despite the larger competitor's marketing spend of 10 million krone (roughly $2 million) each year, iProspect saw an opening. The Norwegian School of Management was utterly absent in organic or paid search.

According to iProspect Norway's managing director, Sander Alten: "The competitor—we couldn't find them on search, either on organic or paid search. We showed our client that this was the way to go. We knew that lots of people would search for this—also, because students only had two months to decide which school to apply to, we knew they would turn to search. We agreed that search was the right thing even though the budget was 50,000 krone—almost nothing!"

The campaign itself focused on three areas. First, they bought keywords associated with the lowest hanging fruit: "study business administration," "study management," "study economics," and so on. Second, they chose to include a local focus, using terms like "study Oslo." Last, they grabbed the specific phrases and curriculum names—the actual names of the classes offered—from their much larger competitor. While avoiding their competitor's brands and copyrights, they leveraged the giant's traditional marketing campaign by borrowing their language.

The four-month campaign, which ran from May through August 2008, drove a 500 percent increase in enrollment from the previous year, beating not only the self-imposed goal of increasing enrollment threefold but even the larger Norwegian School of Management's enrollment by nearly double.

The campaign itself was successful for many reasons. With literally no competition online and a compressed timeframe for prospective students to make their decisions, clicks themselves were not only relatively cheap. but the click-through rates were a relatively high 33 percent. Oslo University's cost per applicant was 5 krone, roughly $0.85. Their competitor, meanwhile, was spending 1,725 krone, or $300, per applicant.

You don't need to be facing a giant who is completely absent from online to apply iProspect's strategy here: Capture your audience's attention at the point of research, skillfully using a keyword strategy that leverages the giant's lingo, and join conversations they thought were closed.

Oslo University shows us an example of smart people taking advantage of the significant marketing investments that others have made and stepping in at that last moment to capture the sale. The key to this strategy is the relationship between online and offline marketing, and the way consumers make up their minds. "We did a research study with Jupiter Research that uncovered that two thirds of all people are driven to perform a search based on being exposed to some form of offline messaging," iProspect CEO Robert Murray explained. "If that adage holds true, then you don't have to be the one to be investing in all that offline messaging. You can be very smart and leverage large media spends that other people have made."

Once you understand that you don't have to be the one to make all the upfront investments in driving traffic, your opportunities are only limited by your imagination and bound by the amount of work you're willing to put in. "Bid on Clydesdales if you're going after Budweiser or geckos if you're going after Geico," Murray told me. "As long as you're not openly misleading people in terms of using brands or brand keywords in your ad copy, you can be very smart about how you go after your competitors."

What enduring lessons can we take away from iProspect's Oslo University campaign?

- **SPENDING DOESN'T EQUAL CONVERSION.** Just because your giant is carpet-bombing the market with its message doesn't mean this will translate into sales. It might translate into awareness, interest, or even intent—but there's plenty of room left for others if the loop isn't properly closed. Find the strategic gaps in the giant's marketing campaign and step in there.

- **WHAT DOES THE CUSTOMER SEE?** What does the customer use? iProspect was the right partner at the right moment for Oslo University because in those waning days before applications were due, the market really had to turn to search. We don't buy college on impulse. We make informed decisions. And in this day and age, we have the online tools available to us to do this easily.

- **TAKE ADVANTAGE OF LOCAL COVER.** This campaign is a strong example of smaller players borrowing the giant's words and traditional market heft to hijack the traffic and convert the sale.

iProspect and Oslo University provide us with a clear story of how a small, nimble brand—with virtually no marketing budget and no time—can be smart and tactical, avoiding the giant's spending while dovetailing nicely with the giant's message.

Key Takeaways

Winning in the Last Three Feet is how smart brands leverage their giants' initiatives and hijack them at the last possible moment, capitalizing on other people's money. This is a strategy that works broadly across many industry types and requires a deep understanding of the process your customer goes through when purchasing the product. Where can you naturally jump into the conversation, and what are they looking to hear before they make the decision?

There's a point in every transaction where your customer is open to suggestion—either actively or passively—and this is where you have to compete. This could be the customer clutching the circular in the aisles of the local store, staring at too many options for the product he thinks he needs. This person could be searching online for that last bit of convincing they need so they can sleep well at night knowing they made a smart decision. The most ready your prospect will ever be is when they've made active decisions to buy a product. So it's our job to never assume the sale is closed.

Authority carries a lot of weight. Real knowledge is often hard to spot, but the trappings of authority are easy. We take the advice of authority figures even when we know what we're supposed to do—even when we know we're not supposed to do what they're suggesting, as a matter of fact. Is there an authority that your customer will listen to before the sale? This could be a salesperson, an influencer, or even a naturally occurring presence in Google search, paid or organic. Some trappings of authority carry more force than others, but it's important to acknowledge that very few of us will casually dismiss what an "expert" is telling us. So leverage your influencers. They can sway a lot of people who in their heart of hearts haven't made up their minds yet.

Create "question marks" where your giant believes they have already put a "period." We're all subject to invidious comparison; our egos get involved in just about everything. If we can play the exclusivity card, if we get a story we can tell our neighbors and coworkers that explains why our esoteric choice was better than theirs, we're happy. We're in an age of smart consumerism. We all want to be seen as knowledgeable and confident in our choices. Consumers want to know something new and buy something their friends don't know about. You have psychology working for you, so let it do its work.

Spend someone else's money. The single most powerful reason to employ the strategy of **Winning in the Last Three Feet** is that it gives you the opportunity to spend someone else's hard-earned money. There's reason to be happy that your giant has the ability to launch large-scale marketing efforts, because they allow you to join a party in progress. They will drive foot traffic—not terribly qualified, open to suggestion—into your arms. If you only close the loop and finish well, you will have met them at precisely the right moment.

CHAPTER FOUR: *Fighting Dirty*

Just because they're bigger than you are doesn't mean you can't pick on them. Is this crazy? No. Just remember that an honest, toe-to-toe fight is the last thing you want. Now is no time for rules.

When you choose to fight dirty, you create match-up problems, launch suicide missions, and embrace misdirection.

Fighting dirty is dangerous. Tread carefully.

The thing about strategic shifting is you need to get to a vantage point where you can look at a problem and see the maximum opportunity . . . where you can shift the odds in your favor. Most people just keep pounding on the same points over and over. If you're able to read the situation—the expected and unexpected patterns, the people—you can do this.

—DR. STEVEN FEINBERG, PSYCHOLOGIST

Dr. Steven Feinberg is a bit of an anomaly: a transplanted New Yorker working and living in Palo Alto, California, and a die-hard Yankees fan deep in the heart of Giants country. His attitudes about life and people reflect a very non–Silicon Valley sensibility.

"I grew up around bookies and others who didn't read books," he explained. "Entrepreneurs who made things happen on the street. My dad was a guy who knew what to say and when to say it to get someone to do something. Looking back, it was usually about me doing something for him."

Feinberg has mentioned his father a lot in our conversations. Feinberg the elder wasn't a PhD in psychology, like his son, but what he knew about people and their motivations served him well—and served as a model for what became his son's calling. "At one point in his life," Feinberg recalled, "he had a small business—an Italian restaurant and pizzeria. I remember that when I was in my late teens, we were in the midst of a pretty big recession. Our family's economic viability was at risk. I was driving around with him and he went to one of his suppliers for the meats and the sauces and the cheeses. It was a hole in the wall, but it pumped out a lot of product. He needed to get lower prices or he couldn't keep the doors open. So he goes into the office and has a conversation with these guys. About twenty minutes later he comes out with a look on this face like things aren't going to work out.

"I'd never seen this look on his face. He walked back in to the meeting. Fifteen minutes later he came back out. He kissed the back of his right hand and kissed the back of his left hand and told me, 'There's no one better than me.' I started laughing. Somehow, he'd shifted the game."

Feinberg's father didn't go to his supplier with hat in hand, begging for lower pricing in a recession. He proposed a solution that would help their flagging demand. Pizza joints were going belly-up all over New York. They were feeling this too. So he made a deal to promote their service to all the other pizzerias in the city. In exchange, he got lower prices. And a loan.

"The thing about strategic shifting is, you need to get to a vantage point where you can look at a problem and see things other people miss," Feinberg explained. "You see how and where you can shift the odds in your favor."

Many people just keep pounding on the same points over and over. They don't question the givens. If you're able to read the situation and see the expected patterns—as well as the unexpected ones—you can begin to see things that tilt the odds in your favor.

WE'RE ALL FACED WITH what may look like insurmountable problems. A competitor may have more money in their petty cash drawer than we have in our total budget and an R&D team larger than our entire company. Competing with giants on an equal footing, under the same assumptions and playing by the same rules, is a losing game. You may go down in glorious flames, but you'll still end up on the floor. So take a page from Dr. Feinberg's book. Shift your perspective.

What vantage point can you climb to survey the field from a different angle? What givens can you question that might upset the balance of power? There are some people who are naturally gifted at strategic shifting. For the rest of us, we can purposefully choose to put these tools to work for us by carefully going through our own series of mental diagnostics. What assumptions am I making? What are the "facts"? What happens when I change them? What patterns of behavior, structure, or timing do I see? Forget my vantage point for a moment: What does this situation look like from my opponent's perspective? What about the people we're both trying to serve—what do they see, or believe, or care about? How do each of these variables impact my options?

Many of these appear to be difficult questions to answer when you're neck deep in a sticky problem, but that's what makes them powerful. Every time we see a stunning example of strategic shifting—particularly when the shift is simple but creates a tremendous effect—we always wonder why we'd never thought of it before.

Fighting Dirty is about making those strategic shifts that no one else can see, turning everything your opponent believes upside-down.

Mutually Assured (Brand) Destruction: Tab Clear Versus Crystal Pepsi

It was a suicidal mission from day one. Pepsi spent an enormous amount of money on the brand and, regardless, we killed it. Both of them were dead within six months.

—SERGIO ZYMAN, FORMER CMO OF COCA-COLA

The early nineties was a meat grinder for the beverage industry— unless you were Snapple, of course, in which case you were riding a rocket. Snapple's meteor-like impact on the U.S. beverage market took volume away from everything else, including the powerhouse colas. This drop in volume had to be dealt with somehow, some way, because shareholders didn't care about the "why" as much as they cared about the "when" of the current management team's fix for the problem. This was a tough time. But tough times spawn interesting ideas. And Crystal Pepsi was an interesting idea.

Read the press from 1992 and you'll see a very confident Pepsi eagerly launching their new product. There was considerable buzz about this new clear, noncaffeinated cola. Many predicted it would be very successful; some predicted it would change the face of colas entirely. Positioned somewhere in the exploding New Age beverage category along with Snapple and other nontraditional drinks but still a cola, Crystal Pepsi was enigmatic and a source of concern for Coca-Cola.

By this point, Sergio Zyman had pretty much seen it all, having been Coke's marketing chief responsible for guiding the company's strategy through the launch of Diet Coke as well as New Coke. Between his two tenures at Coca-Cola, and shortly before he returned to the company as its first chief marketing officer, Sergio was consulting with the company on a number of strategic issues and watching this unfolding drama at Pepsi closely. "Pepsi had decided to launch a clear cola," he told me. "So Pepsi said, 'If we launch a cola, which is the bulk of the market, that is clear, then we can capture a large percent of the market.' They wanted to launch it at the Super Bowl. They kind of got carried away with it."

While studying the competitive intelligence, Zyman saw an opening—and executed a strategic shift. "What I found was that, when I did the research, one of the critical attributes that was coming through was the whole idea that clarity conveyed wellness." He realized that "a way to ambush Crystal Pepsi is to do a kamikaze on them—commit suicide and kill them in the process. So I went to the company and sold them on the idea."

Crystal Pepsi had some confusing attributes, to be sure. Clear meant "wellness" to consumers and the product's caffeine-free formulation supported this impression. But its clear formulation made it visually similar to the lemon-lime category, even though it was a full-fledged cola. And while clear may suggest wellness to consumers, Crystal Pepsi wasn't a diet drink. There was plenty to be confused about. So Zyman led the charge to reposition the competition and make sure the confusion was known to everyone.

"What we did is we said we would launch a Tab Clear product and position it right next to Crystal Pepsi, and we'd kill both in the process," he told me. "We basically repositioned the competition." Tab Clear's launch, with its legacy of being a second-tier diet drink and its overlapping position of being clear, further muddied the already confusing image of Crystal Pepsi in the mind of the market. It validated the clear beverage market— but with a deadly twist: The validation was coming from a brand perceived to be far below the status and cache of the flagship Pepsi product and one that was clearly cemented in the minds of the public as a diet entry. Like a new fad too quickly adopted by the uncool members of the class, Crystal Pepsi's luster took an instant hit.

"They were going to basically say it was a mainstream drink," Zyman continued. "This is like a cola, but it doesn't have any color. It has all this great taste. And we said, 'No, Crystal Pepsi is actually a diet drink.' Even though it wasn't. Because Tab had the attributes of diet, which was its demise. That was its problem. It was perceived to be a medicinal drink. Within three or five months, Tab Clear was dead. And so was Crystal Pepsi."

To many industry watchers, the launch of Tab Clear was a failure—a clear cola, a me-too product weakly launched against a juggernaut. But if its mission was to stick to Crystal Pepsi and drag both products down, it succeeded beautifully.

"It was a suicidal mission from day one," Zyman explained. "Pepsi spent an enormous amount of money on the brand and, regardless, we killed it. Both of them were dead within six months."

Tab Clear gives us an excellent example of carefully sabotaging your competitor's flagship launch with the smart positioning of a drab market entry. What lessons can we take from this story?

- **NO ONE WANTS TO STAND NEXT TO THE CLOWN.** Everybody ends up looking like they deserve a red ball on their noses. Think of a presidential debate where too many people are up on stage. Everyone is trying to look "presidential," but they can't. There's too much going on and the one guy who talks funny keeps making the audience laugh. In the end, everyone ends up looking silly. The debate ends in a draw. Everybody loses.

- **DON'T GIVE YOUR COMPETITOR THE VALIDATION IT DESIRES.** If Coke had launched a clear version of flagship Coca-Cola brand, we'd all be sipping some sort of clear cola today. We're not. Coke played its cards right, sending a slightly worn, very unsexy brand out to make both of them look foolish. In the process, they sunk both—on purpose.

- **WE CAN MOVE THE MARKET'S ANCHOR POINTS BY SUBTLE BUT IMPORTANT DEGREES WITH THE CAREFUL PLACEMENT OF OUR OWN COMPETITIVE PRODUCTS.** This strategy works better in more subjective, lower involvement products than many others, but the underlying truth still holds up to scrutiny. When we're dealing with subjectivity—in matters of personal taste—this strategy makes sense. Where emotional attachment to a brand, a product, or an idea is at stake, Tab Clear's self-destructing strategy is deadly.

Tab Clear's strategy was to muddy the already murky waters and make the entire category look less sexy than Pepsi planned for it to be. By bringing the entire market segment down to a less sexy, quasi-medicinal pall, Tab Clear sank clear cola. Both ended up dead within the year, which was the point all along.

One Plus One Equals #1:
Searle Canada's Arthrotec

It's one of those ideas that seemed perfectly obvious in hindsight. If you're a physician prescribing a nonsteroidal anti-inflammatory drug, you know in your heart of hearts that these things cause problems, but you're never going to admit it. Our experience in marketing Cytotec was that if we tried to do a frontal assault, it was going to be an issue because we're trying to convince doctors that they're doing something wrong. So this oblique approach was one that gave them legitimacy and made it OK to talk about.

—RICHARD HINSON, FORMER PRESIDENT AND
GENERAL MANAGER OF SEARLE CANADA

First, do no harm.

This is a tall order when you're prescribing pain medication to an arthritis sufferer. The painkillers may work, but they do a number on your stomach. They cause ulcers, which are often as bad as or worse than the arthritis you are trying to treat. In the early nineties, pharmaceutical company Searle developed a molecule that protected patients' stomachs and prevented the ulcers, but convincing Canada's doctors that they were doing something wrong struck CEO Richard Hinson as something akin to pushing a rope uphill. So instead of just pushing harder, he and his team at Searle Canada changed the rules and won a different game.

Searle's Cytotec drug was designed to protect the patient's stomach lining from the harmful side effects of nonsteroidal anti-inflammatory drugs (NSAIDs) used to relieve arthritis pain. Doctors therefore had to write two prescriptions—one to deal with the pain and the other to deal with the painkiller. Rather than try to convince doctors that they were harming patients by prescribing NSAIDs without Cytotec, Searle simply combined Cytotec with a generic NSAID in one compound to make a one-pill solution:

Arthrotec. This new drug wasn't an anti-ulcer drug that you took with your anti-inflammatory—it was a better anti-inflammatory that didn't cause ulcers. A simple, game-changing difference.

"You have to be brutally honest about what your marketplace sees and how they approach things," Hinson told me. "Admitting that doctors won't want to be hit over the head with the idea that they're hurting their patients . . . was really the heart of our oblique approach."

Arthrotec's launch in 1997 was accelerated by a thought-leader campaign representing another strategic shift, this one relying on what could adequately be called enlightened self-interest. So much of market acceptance comes down to momentum. When everyone else is running in one direction, it's hard not to feel the gravitational pull of your peers. Searle created a stampede in the medical community by sponsoring a one-million-dollar grant for anyone who could invent a way to diagnose early-stage ulcers from NSAID use. In short, they "declared the debate over" and shined a very bright light on the problems of NSAIDs taken without the protective benefit of Cytotec. "We weren't necessarily interested in a device or a protocol—we wanted to publicize the fact that NSAIDs gave you ulcers and stomach problems. We supported this with a major media push. We had enormous response to this from medical schools. It gave us enormous amounts of publicity, well over the million-dollar investment." It's tough for a doctor to stand idly by while the rest of the medical community is scrambling to prove that non-Arthrotec NSAIDs were causing ulcers.

As a result of these two strategic shifts, Arthrotec became the leading arthritis drug and one of the top twenty prescribed drugs in all of Canada, taking Searle from zero to number one in the category.

What can a careful reader learn from Arthrotec?

- **AN INSIDER WOULD SAY THIS IS UNFAIR.** "They just combined the anti-inflammatory with the anti-ulcer drug. It's just like our stuff, but they put it together." And while they'd be right, they'd be missing the point. A doctor would say this is better. And a patient would say this is the one I want even if I have to pay for it out of my own pocket.

- **CONVINCING PEOPLE THEY'RE WRONG IS DIFFICULT.** Giving them the means to do what they're already doing a little bit better is easier.

- **NO ONE SELLS A PEER LIKE A PEER.** When all your colleagues are scrambling to prove that the debate is over, most people end up following along. The grant strategy ethically tapped the medical community's enlightened self-interest, driving awareness, compliance, and ultimately acceptance of the product the way that no public relations campaign could ever have done on its own.

Searle Canada's Arthrotec launch gives us a great example of doing what looks obvious after the fact but in reality was a brilliant strategic shift. Searle questioned all of the givens and succeeded where others would have predicted failure.

Wrestling with the Proverbial Pig: Hershey's Krackel Versus Nestlé Crunch

The more he looked at it, the more he got this smile on his face. He said this is a pretty evil plot. The big guy can't win on this and we can't lose. It boosted all of our sales because it got us into a lot of doors. This helped our business across the board.

—STEVE MULLEN, FORMER KRACKEL BRAND MANAGER, HERSHEY

Sometimes, the giant you face is so big, you need to look up just to see the bottoms of their shoes. Imagine facing a competitor's flagship product from a position as a bottom-tier brand so small you literally have no above-the-line marketing budget at all. Now, your job is to go out there and take a chunk out of your giant's hide.

That's pretty much the story that marketer Steve Mullen told me when he looked back on his days running Hershey's Krackel brand in the eighties. Krackel was a 17-million-dollar brand facing a behemoth, Nestlé's $150-million Crunch franchise. "We literally had no spending budget," Mullen told me. "It didn't justify any financial support whatsoever." When viewed from this perspective, it doesn't seem like Mullen and Krackel had much of a chance to do anything significant to upset the balance of power in this marketplace. What was needed was a different perspective, and in April of 1985, Mullen quickly found the vantage point he needed, beginning with his choice of the vending machine class of trade, a relatively quiet backwater channel that represented roughly 7 percent of Hershey's total volume.

Your typical candy bar vending machine has thirty to fifty slots, and the vending distributors who keep them stocked and determine their in-machine assortments don't like to dedicate two slots to the same category of candy bar. So either you get the slot or your competitor does. This was a zero-sum, all-or-nothing proposition. And Krackel at that moment was a nonentity in vending with absolutely nothing to lose.

"There's a limit to how much you can usually put behind a brand in trade support, but in Krackel's case it didn't have anything," Mullen told me. "It struck me that if we got our discounts down deep enough, one of two things would happen. One is that either the trade would de-list Nestlé from all of their vending machines just because Krackel would be so much more profitable—and the consumer didn't differentiate that much between brands. The other was that Nestlé would have to meet our discounts. Either Krackel would pick up more facings—the number of slots that the bar would occupy—or Nestlé would have to fork up so many dollars that they would take money away that they might use to support other brands, too. So it was a win-win."

Mullen's proposal to management was to give the vending distributors a 30 percent trade discount on Krackel where other brands hovered in the 5 to 10 percent range. This was understandably a bold move. "I originally took it to my boss and he choked on it. He said we couldn't afford it. Giving away thirty points was a big deal. I said, 'Think of the options. If Nestlé tries to match us, the dollar cost to them is huge. That, or we blow Krackel out in every vending machine in the country.'" With nothing to lose—and aiming at the brand that paid for so many of its chief competitor's other brands—Krackel could play the role of spoiler. "My boss balked at it at first, but the more he looked at it, the more he got this smile on his face. He said this is a pretty evil plot. The big guy can't win on this and we can't lose."

Krackel launched across the country with its jaw-dropping trade discount, forcing Nestlé to meet this unexpected threat with a similar discount across the base of its entire Crunch volume in the vending class of trade. But that didn't last. Not only did it drain the discretionary spending budgets across their entire company to fund this unanticipated attack, but Nestlé's major national accounts—their big customers in the grocery and mass merchant channels—soon learned of this new corporate largesse that apparently was not mentioned in their last most-favored-nations pricing meetings. So this temporary discount aimed at dealing with an inconsequential competitor in an inconsequential class of trade threatened to cascade across the entire base of Nestlé's business. Once the pain was too great, Nestlé folded, leaving Krackel as the last bar standing and boosting the brand's revenue by an incremental $25 million. More than that, it provided an entry point for other Hershey products into the vending class, riding the coattails of this once lowly brand.

What can we take away from Krackel?

- **IT'S NOT ABOUT SIZE OR BUDGET OVERALL; IT'S ABOUT LEVERAGE IN ONE SPOT.** The vending class of trade was the proverbial "pinky finger" of the $150-million Nestlé Crunch brand, and Krackel twisted it hard.

- **IF YOU CAN'T COMPETE ON MARKETING SPENDING, COMPETE ON PAIN THRESHOLDS.** Krackel couldn't compete on above-the-line, traditional marketing investment. But by virtue of its small size—and relative unimportance to the overall Hershey P&L—it could win on the basis of having a higher pain threshold.

- **HALO EFFECTS HAVE FAR-REACHING CONSEQUENCES.** Look at what this program did in a short period of time, from driving incremental volume for Krackel, to allowing other Hershey products to ride its coattails, to sapping Nestlé's marketing dollars across all brands and channels, to even threatening to cascade this deep discount into other more important classes of trade. This program did a lot of good and put more than just a small portion of Nestlé's business at risk.

Krackel's trade discount—an inconsequential brand in an inconsequential class of trade—made giant Nestlé dance to their tune, temporarily upsetting the status quo in a business dominated by big budgets.

This isn't a strategy for everyone. But it does give us reason to look for areas of relative advantage, where localized efforts can have wide-reaching consequences. If we can force the giant's hand, we've achieved a strategic victory.

Key Takeaways

Fighting Dirty is how smart brands create match-up problems for their larger competitors, making them fight where they don't want to fight and using tactics they find difficult to counter. What key takeaways can we extract from these companies?

Look at your battlefield from a different perspective. Dr. Steven Feinberg's concept of strategic shifting is a valuable tool for choosing the right approach to tackle a difficult competitive threat. How can you view the battlefield from a different angle? A new perspective can make all the difference.

Question the givens. One of the greatest tools we have at our disposal is our ability to judiciously question what we at first assume to be unquestionable. What do you think is absolutely, positively, irreversibly true? Now look at ways to make this immovable object a variable. What has just changed in your calculus? What do you need to do, or learn, to make this given a variable? It may seem like mental gymnastics, but you will quickly uncover opportunities that stop your competitors. It's worth the effort.

Question the structures. Look for combinations where others see only stand-alone solutions. Who says an anti-ulcer drug can't become the bestselling anti-inflammatory in Canada? Only those who fail to see it as a potential component instead of a finished product. Who says the humble vending machine segment can't be the lever that upsets the entire industry structure? Question the structures of your business and look for new ways to recombine the pieces and present new solutions.

Tap your market's sense of "enlightened self-interest." Arthrotec's million-dollar grant positioned the battle as already won, getting independent thought leaders to stampede in their efforts to validate the company's core business proposition. Imagine the resistance to the same message delivered via traditional means. How can you tap game theory and play to your audience's desires? If you create conditions under which "the debate is over," will it end the debate?

How can we avoid validating our competitor? Crystal Pepsi didn't want to have to share the spotlight with Tab any more than Nestlé Crunch wanted to have to compete head to head against Krackel. Much like knights in shining armor, giants seek out other similarly upper crust opponents for a dignified challenge and shy away from the deadly archers and infantry who might unhorse them dishonorably. Both giants were forced to appear with less than noble adversaries with no glory to win in the contest. As a result, both had to abandon their carefully constructed plans and fight in the mud, to everyone's delight but theirs.

Remember that it's not about how they look to you—it's also about how you look to them. You might see a giant with massive budgets and unlimited resources. They might see a scrappy competitor with nothing to lose. Both are daunting. The playing field might be more level than you thought. Instead of looking up at your giant and feeling intimidated by its size, think of how your giant must be viewing you, wondering what they stand to lose. The mouse fears the elephant and the elephant fears the mouse.

CHAPTER FIVE: *Eat the Bug*

Some parts of the giant's culture and worldview are so essential to their self-image that they can't bring themselves to even question them. Often, these aren't even things the company can articulate. They are just givens. We do things like this and would never do things like that.

This dark corner is where opportunity resides. Learn to love what the giant considers taboo. Be willing to do what they aren't and build a business out of it, every day.

Go ahead. Do the unthinkable. Eat the bug.

It's absolutely ingrained in human nature that we simply assign responsibility for what went wrong instead of chalking it up to bad luck. And bad luck is out there. You can't totally insulate yourself from it because if you try to, you really impair your ability to achieve good luck. And unfortunately, the world is sufficiently complex that you have to make the conditional assumption that you're going to get some breaks along the line. Otherwise, you're dead.

—BOB HAMMAN, WORLD'S NUMBER-ONE-RANKED BRIDGE PLAYER

Bob Hamman can tell you the odds of an average spectator taking a basketball and sinking a half-court shot depending on whether the sports fan in question knows ahead of time that he's going to have the chance or whether he's called out of the stands without warning. (Hint: Having time to practice matters a lot.) When you want to run that "million-dollar hole-in-one" fund-raiser, Hamman is the guy you'd turn to so you can sleep well at night. When Pepsi ran their national promotion that offered to give away a billion dollars, Hamman handled the risk through his company, SCA Promotions. And, as the world's top-ranked bridge player, Hamman has a finely tuned understanding of risk tolerance and game theory.

Taking the risk out of risky business is what Hamman does, professionally and for fun, so his comments on risk tolerance are particularly insightful. "There's a bias toward deferring to the most conservative course of action in an organization when you're looking to get authorization for something—that's just the way it is, not good, not bad," Hamman told me. "Even if you get the multiple sign-offs required and something goes sideways, human nature comes to the fore and memories get short. We like to assign responsibility for what went wrong instead of chalking it up to bad luck. And bad luck is out there." It's reassuring to know that not everything is our fault. Bad luck is out there, regardless of the inevitable tendency of many company cultures to rush to judgment and quickly lay blame for projects that go astray.

It's not just the size of the company that determines risk tolerance either. Even the size of the group making the decision weighs on the group's tolerance for uncertainty. "This dynamic of decisions getting more complicated the more people are involved is good in some cases. You don't want a hothead going to war over a minor transgression. On the other hand, if all you've got to lose is money you can afford to lose, taking a reasonable economic risk is sensible. You have to act on the information you have available, draw conclusions, and get on with life."

Assessing the risk of a large-scale marketing investment is no different than assessing the hand you've been dealt at the table. "Take poker. You call the bet, fold, or raise. It's all a real-time appraisal of your position and the constraints of your bankroll and what you think the real value is. In appraising equity, you really have to distinguish between what you want to be the case and what the case really is. The winds of fate don't really care. They're not rooting for you or against you. If you can be fairly dispassionate about your situation, you can improve your chances. I've screwed up so many situations. I want to believe. Because I like the good feelings when I win. And I'm fairly insensitive to the bad feelings when I lose."

Risk tolerance is a double-edged sword, of course. You can't win if you don't play. "You can't totally insulate yourself from bad luck because if you try to, you really impair your ability to achieve good luck," Bob told me. "And unfortunately, the world is sufficiently complex that you have to make the conditional assumption that you're going to get some breaks along the line. Otherwise, you're dead."

ASSIGNING BLAME FOR FAILED projects is an art form in most large organizations, a specialized behavior that emerged through extreme competition for the increasingly scarce resource of senior-level jobs. It's a well-traveled adage that senior managers in large companies are the guys who are paid to say no to risky ideas. In a sense, they exist to fear change and resist it at all costs. And when they're all together, they get even worse.

View this idea through the lens of the psychology of influence and we can attribute this to what we'd call "loss-based framing"—we feel the pain of losses more acutely than we do the pleasure of gains. This psychological principle becomes amplified with each additional person involved and with the increasing size of the company. The larger the company, the more there is to lose. We all have a psychological tendency to squirrel away our winnings.

When we're betting with nothing, however, the rules change. We have nothing to lose.

View this idea through the lens of game theory and we see what we'd call an asymmetrical game of chicken, with a few important twists. When playing chicken, the best outcome is for you to compete and for your opponent to cooperate; James Dean keeps driving while the other guy swerves out of his way. In our game, the giant really just wants the challenger to go away so it can fight the battles it has already planned to fight on its to-do list for the day. But the giant-killer would like nothing more than the validation—and the chance to win—that such a fight would present. Even in losing, the challenger comes out slightly ahead. Winning the fight, however, is a big win—and a catastrophic loss for the giant.

When we do what the giant simply can't afford to do, whether for structural, branding, or risk reasons, we force them to do what they find unthinkable—and they usually opt not to fight at all.

Going (Barefoot) Where Giants Fear to Tread: Vibram's FiveFingers Running Shoe

Almost everybody in the beginning was repulsed by them, I'd have to say. Even when we showed them to customers, they'd say, "Those are interesting . . . but they're very ugly." And frankly we got better at it. Lots of people still find it highly controversial.

—TONY POST, CEO OF VIBRAM USA

Everyone has the same reaction the first time they see a pair of Vibram FiveFingers shoes, and while the actual words may vary, the sentiment is always the same. Everyone agrees that the shoe, with its individual "fingers" for the wearer's toes, is interesting; they're just not sure it's for them, personally.

Our style choices help define who we are to other people, so those who gravitate to aesthetically risky athletic shoes like these are a select group with some very strong ideas about fitness and individuality. But for those who suffer from the increasingly prevalent injuries that runners get from repeated heel striking, the FiveFingers shoe is a breakthrough. Its beginnings, however, were anything but a sure thing.

Vibram USA's CEO, Tony Post, described the company's shift from its roots as a pure OEM supplier of outer soles to becoming a player in the branded athletic shoe market. "There weren't very many case studies for us, frankly, when we went into this," he recalled. At the time, "component makers who went into the branded business" were a rarity. The company had embarked on a long-term plan to revitalize the seventy-year-old brand by making the company's outer soles more relevant to a younger and broader base of business, forging relationships with brands like Burton snowboards, Shimano mountain bike shoes, UGG boots, and others. The company's next goal was to tap into the highly competitive athletic shoe market, looking for a way to boost innovation in the staid and increasingly commoditized sole business, even to the point of potentially launching their own finished product. But while all options were on the table, the goal was clear. Vibram had no interest in launching a me-too product.

"The opportunity we saw was that although billions had been spent in product research and development, people were still getting injured," Post explained. "Eventually, if people run enough, they tend to get injured and they have pain or they have to stop." The goal, then, was to discover a solution that would enable runners to keep running without pain. And at this critical point of the story, a young shoe designer named Robert Fliri appeared in Milan, pitching a completely unique idea to the shoe establishment and catching the attention of Vibram's Chairman, Marco Bramani.

"Originally, FiveFingers was developed by a young design student in Italy who was an outdoorsman and a naturalist who understood the benefits of being barefoot, living in a rocky area near the Dolomites in Italy," marketing manager Georgia Shaw explained to me. "He developed the idea of FiveFingers as his senior thesis." Fliri's prototype caught Vibram precisely at the right moment. "We were in the midst of the athletic shoe launch when we stumbled onto Robert's idea and we quickly did a U-turn," Post said.

The arrival of the FiveFingers concept was more than just a product launch for Post, a competitive runner facing difficult decisions after knee surgery. "My surgeon told me to give up running, which wasn't the reason I had the surgery to begin with," he explained. "Out of desperation, I tried running in these silly little shoes we were developing with Robert. I had run out of options. Believe it or not, the first run I took, I didn't have knee pain. I thought, 'Well, either my knee is getting better or something is different.' The next day, I switched back to my running shoes and the knee pain was back. The next day, back to FiveFingers. What I noticed is that with FiveFingers I can't run on my heel. I have to run on the ball of my foot. I have to land on the ball of my foot. As a result, I no longer experience that impact that runs up my leg and into my knee, so that knee pain is really going away. I knew that there was something quite unique here. All of a sudden, I really became a believer. That changes the nature of things. Once you have that absolute belief—that I knew I wasn't the only person going through that—I knew we could solve problems for lots of people."

The Vibram team took the FiveFingers prototype to its major prospects and customers, looking to sell the idea as an OEM concept. The reactions were unanimously negative. "It's the typical thing that big companies see," Post told me. "All the problems." There were no takers. And with a business plan to enter the athletic shoe market on the whiteboard—and a truly innovative, if somewhat quirky, product in their hands—Vibram realized that their answer was right in front of them. FiveFingers became the company's first branded shoe, enabling them to enter the athletic shoe category with a breathtakingly original product, all without endangering their established OEM relationships.

Sales volumes at first were modest. "Our first year we had twenty-four accounts and we did 85 to 90 percent of our volume online, direct to consumers," Post told me. "It was the consumers who went into retail shops and asked for them. We've never taken out an ad. It's all been grown by word of mouth. Before long, it was the stores coming to us saying, OK, send a sales rep. Something's happened." Customers gravitated to this new shoe with its minimalist design. "Go to our Facebook site and you'll read what consumers say about us—we have forty-five to fifty thousand fans," Post told me. "It's an odd thing. People have developed this emotional connection to it. I think we really created a category of footwear that, whether you call it natural running or natural fitness, it's allowing the body to move in a more natural way," Post explained.

What can a careful reader learn from Vibram FiveFingers?

- **YOU CAN COMPETE WITH YOUR OWN CUSTOMERS AS LONG AS YOU DO SOMETHING THEY CAN'T IMAGINE DOING THEMSELVES.** Vibram pitched the product to its customers first, defusing any potential problems downstream.

- **WHO ELSE WOULD LAUNCH A "BAREFOOT" RUNNING SHOE BUT A COMPANY KNOWN FOR INNOVATIONS IN SHOE SOLE DESIGN?** It makes sense that Vibram, for those familiar with the brand, to create such a product. You can do what the giant can't by taking on audacious projects that would make sense for you but not for them. Vibram launching a truly innovative product based on a shoe sole is believable to the market—and it pushes the giant to a condition where not competing is a more comfortable option.

- **DO WHAT THEY CAN'T, OR WON'T, DO.** This lesson isn't just for OEM suppliers looking for ways to sell finished goods. It holds true for any brand that exists in the shadow of a larger channel partner whose size and relative market strength threatens to overwhelm them.

- **BIG COMPANIES REWARD THEIR EMPLOYEES NOT FOR TAKING RISKS BUT FOR AVOIDING THEM.** Post's point that his customers saw the things that big companies typically see—"all the problems"—is telling. But his end users—those runners with knee pain, the barefoot enthusiasts, and the few who have experienced what Tony experienced—saw what it could do and built the brand by word of mouth. A large branded shoe company would dismiss this opportunity as too small. For Vibram, it was ideal.

- **THE FIVEFINGERS SHOE, WITH ITS INDIVIDUAL FINGERS AND MINIMALIST SOLE THICKNESS, WOULD BE INCOMPATIBLE WITH EVERYTHING AN ESTABLISHED ATHLETIC SHOE BRAND STOOD FOR.** The Harvard University research and cover stories touting the physiological benefits of barefoot running suggests that there's more to FiveFingers than novelty. If a major athletic shoe company embraced the FiveFingers design, it would be an explicit admission that their billions of dollars of research and development—not to mention advertising—was misguided and that using their products will eventually injure your knees. Minimalist barefoot running, where you run on the balls of your feet, is incompatible with over-engineered shoes that teach you to run on your heels. The FiveFingers shoe would be an impossible product for a major shoe company to launch.

Vibram and its FiveFingers athletic shoe is a perfect example of doing the unthinkable—creating a shoe so outlandish in its appearance that major brands shy away and so revolutionary in its design that these same brands would have to rethink everything they are and do. It is a product that would invalidate the years of trust and equity that the major players have built. And in doing so, it has insulated itself from criticism for entering into finished goods as well as established a well-defended beachhead for itself from which to grow. If you're an OEM supplier and you're looking for a role model to base your ambitions for brand-building and market expansion, Vibram is leading the way.

Thriving Where Giants Can't Survive: Oi Mobile

Anytime you're the third player you don't have a lot of time. You have to be aggressive.

—PAULINO BARROS, FORMER PRESIDENT OF BELLSOUTH INTERNATIONAL

Pricing your product lower than the competition's can be a slippery slope, particularly when they have deeper pockets than you do. You might gain quick traction with the most price-sensitive customers looking for the best price today, only to lose them to the next big deal that comes along tomorrow. Price wars rarely signal that good times are just around the corner. But Oi Mobile entered the Brazilian mobile telephony market in 2002 aiming squarely at the underserved rural and smaller urban markets with a no-frills prepaid cellular service at a price anyone—even those with "pocket problems"—could afford. But this wasn't a contest of wills to see who could survive longer on lower margins: Oi knew it could live on a lower average revenue per user (ARPU) because its unique structure allowed it to.

Oi Mobile came into being when landline telephone provider Telemar saw the opportunity to break out of the flat growth of its legacy business and buy a cellular license. This would allow it to compete with the incumbent providers who had staked out their claims to the major metro areas with service aimed at the enterprise market. The mobile market was ready to surge, with only 20 percent penetration of Brazil's 190 million potential users. But the mass market wasn't going to be able to step up to the prices offered by the incumbents. These were working-class people and students looking for a simple, cost-effective, prepaid solution. And no one was talking to them.

Oi launched as a pragmatic, affordable brand for those who didn't have a lot of disposable income. They weren't hip. They were down to earth, simple, and practical. It was an entry-level strategy: Sign up with Oi for prepaid cellular services and then, over time, migrate up to landline telephony and maybe even broadband. But first, Oi had to position itself carefully to this no-nonsense prepaid market. "We decided that the mobile management would be a different company with a different brand," Oi's customer relationship director, Maxim Medvedovsky, told me. "At that time, the mobile operators in Brazil didn't have strong brands. They had this feeling of being state-owned companies. We were inspired by what Orange did in the UK, so we decided to make a new brand oriented to the mass market. We were the first mobile operator that didn't have any reference to being a telecommunications company. We created Oi, which in Portuguese means 'hi.' We also wanted to be associated with younger customers, not the old incumbent clients."

Coming into the market late had advantages. The first wave of the cellular spectrum auction came with a huge amount of foreign investment in plant and manufacturing, which Oi was able to piggyback on. It's important to note that being the only Brazilian mobile provider operating in Brazil was an additional advantage in that it wasn't focused on foreign exchange fluctuations, as other international firms were. To put this in perspective, in 2002 the dollar was at 2.54 Brazilian reals. When President Lula da Silva began gaining traction, it went up to four, and many foreign players were pleading to get out of the country. Oi escaped all of this.

"They got into the game after the bleeding edge and after the expensive stuff," former BellSouth International President Paulino Barros told me. "We spent almost $3 billion at Bell South. They didn't have to make a huge expenditure, with most of their production being done locally and with lots of financing available. They structured themselves in a way that allowed them to take a very small ARPU so their cost base was aligned to that."

Oi's structural advantages weren't merely the result of leveraging other investments made by those first in the market. Medvedovsky explained, "We were the first GSM player in Brazil. This was important because we had a new technology and a portfolio of handsets with more variety of handsets than our competitors had, and also international roaming. As GSM had over 75 percent of the world volume, we were able to buy handsets at a cheaper price, maybe 20 percent lower price than our CDMA competitors were using at that time. This helped us achieve a higher penetration in the mass market."

Another element in Oi's early years that impacted its ability to price its services where it did was its promotional strategy. The company launched a consumer promotion in 2003 that offered free weekend calling for the first half million customers who signed up for Oi's service for thirty-one years—thirty-one being the area code of Oi's first market in the Belo Horizonte area. More than four million people subscribed during this promotion, hoping to be one of Oi's "pioneers."

Over the next several years, the company faced several new challenges and was forced to continually adapt its strategy. A consolidation of mobile, landline, and broadband services under one umbrella served to give the company a unique selling proposition in the face of competitive moves to copy Oi's success. With GSM-based consumer-oriented mobile rebranding efforts bringing competitors Claro and Vivo to the Brazilian market, Oi's focus on selling bundled services gave it the means to capitalize on the early growth and volume its mobile business had achieved. In 2008, Oi acquired Brazil's second largest fixed landline provider, Brasil Telecom, extending its reach nationally and becoming the country's largest telecommunication company.

What can we take away from Oi Mobile?

- **IDENTIFY WHAT YOUR COMPETITOR IS STRUCTURALLY INCAPABLE OF DOING—BUT YOU ARE.** What do structural advantages allow you to do? If you have a deep field sales force and they rely on e-commerce, you can do face-to-face, in-person evangelism and training on a daily basis, and they can't. If you have an e-commerce model and they have a deep field sales force, chances are you have a lower cost structure that they can't afford to match. Know how far is too far for your competitor and see where this allows you to go.

- **COMPETING ON STRUCTURE MEANS YOU NEED UNARGUABLE ADVANTAGES.** In Oi's case, using a low-cost, no-nonsense, prepaid pricing model wasn't a marketer's idea—it was the heart and soul of the company, rooted in the demographic realities of its customer base and stemming from the company's financial cost structure.

- **IF YOU CAN COMPETE ON STRUCTURE, DON'T BE SHY ABOUT IT.** Everything, from Oi's tagline—"Simple Like That"—to their pricing, their communications, and their brand positioning all stemmed from their structural ability to offer the most competitive prices.

Where such structural differences exist, we always have the opportunity to explore ways of turning them to our advantages— and in Oi's case, this was the ability to live with a lower average revenue per user. Oi's early planning and execution allowed it to capitalize on structural advantages that pushed it to the forefront of Brazil's mobile telephony market, presenting us with a clear example of doing what the giant can't do because of intractable structural issues.

Calling the Ad Agency's Bluff: Cricket Holdings

The P&L guys at the agencies are going to be up at night because now they're going to have to bet their own money. They've never bet their own money before. They bet the client's money. Let's see how they like that game.

—VICTOR GRILLO, CEO AND FOUNDER, CRICKET

Everyone wants to get paid for their work, but not everyone has the confidence to turn the tables and get paid purely on the value of their results. Look at this from a demand-generation perspective. For the buyer, this is a great deal: It allows him to bank on the cost of customer acquisition up front. This saves the buyer a lot of time and effort and helps alleviate the stress of the CEO bursting into his office demanding to know the cost of acquiring one more customer. The seller, on the other hand, has to be very sure that they can produce the results they're offering—because if they can't, their financial world will quickly go upside down.

Cricket Holdings is a direct-response television production company, an agency that produces television commercials that drive interested consumers to make an immediate purchase through a phone call or a Web site visit. If you've ever heard of the Ginsu Knife, Tripledge Wiper Blades, or the Contour Pillow, you've seen Cricket's work. CEO and founder Victor Grillo is quick to point out that direct response isn't necessarily for everyone. "Take a middle-tier brand with a limited advertising budget of maybe $5 to $10 million, where the efficient use of that media will dramatically affect the P&L of that company. Where the efficient use of media is relevant to the business model and the ability to generate revenue from their media expenditures is important to them, direct response is exactly where the client should be." There are a host of traditional agencies in business today who claim proficiency in direct response, and even more pure direct-response agencies to serve these middle-tier clients who want every marketing dollar to count. There are very few, however, who operate on a "pay per lead" basis, selling their clients qualified customers one at a time, and this is what makes Cricket worth discussing.

Cricket began more than twenty years ago, selling products on television that Grillo himself developed or sourced. "Cricket was founded right out of school for me—midway through college," he explained. "We started out in the business of selling widgets and gadgets to consumers on television. We'd take an item, we'd make a TV commercial, we'd run a piece of media, and we'd sell it. We got lucky early—which was lucky because I didn't have too many bullets in the gun at that point." When a major retailer approached him about carrying one of Cricket's "made for TV" products, Grillo realized that his ads were doing more than just selling products on television—they were building a brand. "We found that the sales at retail were ten times what we were selling on TV. It was the tail wagging the dog. What we thought would be ancillary sales became the primary income source of the company. We were creating a brand basically for free, because we were generating enough revenue from TV to not only offset the media expense but to actually turn a profit. We didn't realize at the time how unique this proposition was."

As Cricket grew, it attracted the attention of third-party brands looking for help, from Motorola and Conair to many of the major Las Vegas casinos. This entrée into the agency world gave the company wide exposure to different product categories and the corresponding media habits of their customers. His new clients' frustrations with the risks of advertising resonated with Grillo, and inspired Cricket's "pay per lead" business model.

Grillo describes his business model this way: "Let's say that it costs you a hundred dollars in media to generate a customer. We said, get out of the way and let us handle it for you. I will deliver the lead—the customer—to you at seventy-five dollars, fixed cost, with me doing all the work. You don't need an army of people supervising your agency for you. I'll do everything. All the risk is on my shoulders. I can give him a result cheaper than he can do it himself and save him all the work of doing it."

Not only did this new way of doing things calm his clients' fears, it also put the competition on the defensive. "This dramatically changes the ad agency and marketing world," Grillo explained, "because clients will become more demanding and say, 'Don't give me the three-martini lunch and the fancy Super Bowl ad, I want to spend fifty bucks for every new customer I get—I don't care how you do it, just give me the result.' This puts the general agency guy in a panic, because now they're being held accountable for results. I'm giving a quantifiable result that is totally on my dime. Now, there's nowhere to run. There's no place to hide."

So how does Cricket do what they do? What do they have that other, similar agencies don't? The answer is a combination of three elements working in harmony: structure, intellectual property, and guts.

Cricket sold Advanced Results Marketing, the division that worked with the Las Vegas casinos and other big brands, to the private equity group owning media giant Mercury Media in 2007. This ongoing relationship allows Cricket to tap into Mercury's $500 million in media buying power. More important, this close relationship allows Cricket to buy spot media on a daily basis very flexibly, so where other agencies buy media up front a quarter in advance, Cricket can evaluate campaign results every day based on performance and subsequently change the campaign schedules every evening to optimize the results for tomorrow's ads. This close-to-real-time feedback mechanism continuously optimizes their client's chances for success based on what's happening right then.

The second ingredient in Cricket's "secret sauce" is their database—"HAL," as it's known in the company. "HAL has the results of every commercial we've ever run on every network by day-part by CPM," Grillo told me. "If I run a commercial on Fox News at two p.m., and it does well, HAL will tell me immediately to go book media on CNN, CNBC, and others because they have comparable cost per thousand viewers, demographic profiles, and we've had comparable results with similar products in the past. This twenty years of history and profiling that's in HAL with millions of pieces of data allows us to quite accurately predict on a go-forward basis what our results will be based on historic results. No one has a database like this. No one has a database with one one-hundredth of what we have."

Last, Cricket draws upon Victor's experience of creating ads that have moved more than a billion dollars worth of product through television media over the past twenty years. Over time, you learn what sells and how the creative needs to come together. With twenty years of creative behind him, Victor attributes a lot of Cricket's success to his sense of what gets people to act. The combination of these three elements gives Cricket the confidence to bet on results with their own money.

Does this approach always win? When there's a national event going on that's pulling eyeballs away from their normal television viewing habits, results often fall short. Of course, if it's a rainy Sunday and everyone is at home watching television, Cricket lands its leads for half the price. "Five to ten percent of the time, in a given schedule in a given week, we're upside down," Grillo confided. "But in aggregate, we win far more than we lose."

Cricket shows us an example of a company in a niche professional service market that leans on multiple structural advantages, by virtue of its in-house decision-support systems and media-buying capabilities, as well as its own personal risk tolerance to do what its competitors can't—and won't—do. What enduring lessons can we take away from Cricket?

- **KNOWLEDGE IS A COMPETITIVE WEAPON.** The ability to bring an organized body of observations and evidence to bear on your decision making can mean the difference between placing a reasonable bet and praying for the results you want.

- **HOW CAN YOU PUT YOUR CUSTOMER'S BIGGEST UNSAID FEAR TO BED?** For the second-tier advertiser managing a tight P&L with no room for error, that fear is, "What will one dollar invested in marketing buy me? What do I have to spend to get my next customer?" Cricket delivers against this fear, doing what few are willing to do—put their own money on the line.

- **WITH RISK—CAREFUL, DELIBERATE RISK—COMES REWARD.** Think about what Cricket does: They have an incentive to drive down acquisition costs, because the cheaper they land the lead, the more money they make. The typical advertising agency, whether direct response or traditional, has absolutely no incentive to do this. As a matter of fact, a traditional agency using a standard mark-up business model has an incentive to increase your costs over time. Think of the impact this philosophical shift has on the buyer of their services.

- **WHEN YOU CAN CONFIDENTLY DO WHAT YOUR COMPETITORS FEAR TO CONSIDER**, you've got a very powerful weapon at your disposal.

Cricket shows us an example of a company that has invested time, effort, and money to ensure their clients' success. They have taken a good deal out of the gambling that would otherwise make a "pay per lead" agency business model as profitable as a coin toss, and in doing so have put other agencies on notice. Knowledge, structure, and guts are powerful advantages.

Key Takeaways

Smart brands **Eat the Bug** when they use their natural advantages—intellectual, structural, financial, logical, and emotional—to do what the giant can't imagine doing. What key takeaways can we extract from these companies?

Think deeply about the places a giant can't go. This isn't a casual conversation, and you often need outsiders, experts, and primary research to help flesh this out in a meaningful way. There are things a giant can't do for structural reasons. There are things a giant can't do for marketing reasons. Think about what defines reality for your giant, because once you've got a strong hypothesis about where the giant simply can't go, you've got a road map to uncontested space.

What can you do that they can't? The flip side of the above argument is thinking deeply about the things you can do that they can't. Where are your unarguable areas of advantage? What self-imposed rules does your giant adhere to that simply don't apply to you? You know, for example, that they are beholden to their channel partners (or their unions, or something else)—and you are not. You can now sell directly to your end users and step up your direct communications, customer education initiatives, and other actions without a competitive response.

What does a giant stand to gain (or lose) by contesting your strategic move? Giants have little to gain by publicly taking on a minor player. You, on the other hand, have everything to gain: publicity, validity, and the sure knowledge that giants don't want this much attention. The court of public opinion tends to side with the underdog.

What does a giant stand to lose by competing with you? The larger the competitor, the more conservative they become— they have more layers of management to make happy, more shareholders to appease, and generally more resources to lose in money and reputation. You have focus, the ability to concentrate your efforts behind what a giant simply wants to go away.

What does the giant's business model depend on? How do they make money? Do they bill on an hourly basis? Are they a capital-intensive business holding significant debt? How does their structure play out in the ways they interact with their customers? How does their structure manifest itself in how they bill their clients? What do their customers think of this? Is there a model that these customers would prefer—and is this something you can do that they can't?

What constitutes "common knowledge" in your giant's mind-set? What defines how they approach their business?

Are their shoes foot-mounted shock absorbers? Are their service plans comprised of chapters upon chapters of fine print? Are their monthly retainers built upon the assumption of mark-ups over cost? Anytime a giant has built an empire on top of a set of assumptions that don't cover all possible outcomes (and they won't), there is wiggle room for alternatives that upset the giant's carefully constructed universe.

G iants are masters of the assumptive close. They assume the sale is theirs, and it shows in their sales processes and their marketing language. They know that no one ever got fired for buying their stuff, and they hope and pray that people don't get wise.

Your job is to be the monkey wrench thrown into what was almost a smooth afternoon. You have an irritating way of making customers think for a moment, realizing that in comparison your offering makes more sense.

So go ahead. Make the inconvenient argument.

It's impossible to talk during a prison siege. You just have to let them vent. You can't talk to them while the fire's burning. You have to let them come down to their normal functioning level. On the other hand, if you're dealing with a depressed person behaving below their normal functioning level, you have to build them up so you can be rational with them. And it works. They can't make a good decision if they're not being rational enough—or emotional enough.

—VICTOR BAZAN, HOSTAGE NEGOTIATOR

Victor Bazan was brought in late, on the sixth day of the prison siege at St. Martin Parish Correctional Center in St. Martinville, Louisiana, after the few dozen rioting Cuban detainees had burned out a bit.

"The Cubans who took it over were so emotionally charged you couldn't talk to them at first," he told me, describing the situation he walked into as the chief negotiator on the scene for the FBI. "They were very disorganized, very vicious. They beat the warden pretty badly and took him hostage. We just had to let them vent. It was only after five days of venting that I talked to them. They were venting all over the other negotiators, though, and I was the last one to talk to them."

Bazan's dispassionate description of what was surely a harrowing experience for everybody—both on the inside as well as the outside of the prison—holds a number of insights into compliance techniques under highly charged conditions of uncertainty. Without a doubt, what he's describing is more emotionally charged than what we'd find in a business setting, but within the chaos of a siege we can begin to understand a few of the moving parts in high-stakes negotiation.

"It's impossible to talk during a prison siege," Bazan explained to me. "You just have to let them vent. You can't talk to them while the fire's burning. You have to let them come down to their normal functioning level. On the other hand, if you're dealing with a depressed person behaving below their normal functioning level, you have to build them up so you can be rational with them. And it works. They can't make a good decision if they're not being rational enough—or emotional enough." Once the other side is at their normal functioning level, the negotiator can shift the conversation away from points of conflict to their core psychological hungers: life, food, sex, comfort, and a return to normalcy, whatever that means to a person who is incarcerated.

"You talk to them in a rational way without being accusatory, without asking any interrogation question—you're just two guys engaging in dialogue. We hit it off in a way the other nego-tiators couldn't. They just weren't ready. They won't make a decision until they're ready."

"I was the last one to speak to them on the phone," Bazan explained, detailing the events of the 1998 riot. "After that, we went face to face. They wouldn't pick up the phone after that." Eventually, the FBI brought the detainee leader's girlfriend and mother to the prison to help end the stalemate. With the inmates in disarray—and after six days of no running water or electricity—the FBI unlocked the doors of the prison and let those who wanted to get out the opportunity to give themselves up.

"The takeover came apart from the inside."

VICTOR BAZAN'S STORY OF the St. Martinville prison siege is a vivid example of the FBI switching the emotional polarity—from rational to emotional or emotional to rational—to defuse and ultimately resolve a hostage situation. It doesn't matter if you're talking to a corporate purchasing officer who doesn't want to work too hard evaluating his options, or a psychopath demand-ing a helicopter to Libya, it's going to come down to your abil-ity to move them off of their established anchor point and throw the psychological switch in their brains that allows your argu-ment to be heard.

Under these conditions of emotional polarity, let's consider the role of price. In general terms, a reasonable person would agree that cheaper isn't always better. We simply have to make more sense. Understand that when you're fighting a giant, you're often at a disadvantage: They have more brand awareness, deeper pockets, perhaps a bigger sales organization, and other natural advantages. So our approach really can't be incremen-tal, because we'll get out-incremental-ed. We need to lay down a pricing strategy that isn't easy to flip over and deconstruct. We need something sticky, something only we can do.

This is a tall order. But by reversing the emotional polarity, we shift the competition into a new frame, one different from their current set of assumptions and preconceptions. *We must shift the rational player to an emotional footing and push an emotional player to think more rationally.* If your customer knows that they'll never get in trouble buying the giant's product— "Nobody ever got fired for buying IBM"—it's our job to push them out of their comfort zone, making them think emotionally and sweeping them up in the momentum of our offer. And when they're caught up in the emotional close of a giant's sweeping sales pitch, it's our job to put the math in front of their eyes, slowing them down and making them understand the rational choice.

Changing the emotional polarity of a situation is a powerful strategy when you're fighting a bigger competitor, because it puts the fight on ground of your choosing.

Moving the Channel from the Emotional to the Rational: Kozy Shack and Return on Inventory Investment

When you're working for P&G, the one thing the trade would always complain about is, "Hey, we don't make any money on you." But what you do make is a lot of inventory turns. So look at the grocery industry in general. The average grocery store makes less than 1 percent margin. If I wanted to invest my money somewhere, would I put it in a grocery store or put it in the bank? With a bank, I'd make about 5 percent. In a grocery store, I'd only make 1 percent, but I'd make that 1 percent every week.

—ROBERT STRIANO, CEO OF KOZY SHACK

I was introduced to return on inventory investment (ROII) by Bob Striano, my then-boss at Sony, by way of a battered yellow sales training binder he had kept from his first job out of college as a sales representative at Procter & Gamble. In it was P&G's bible on ROII, spelling out the various ways of calculating it— always the same calculation, just using different ways of getting to it, depending on the data you had on hand—and its various applications.

ROII shows your buyer the profit he or she makes on each dollar they invest in stocking your product over the course of a year. And given a little competitive intelligence into how much your retailer is marking up your giant's products and how fast it is selling—both bits of knowledge that a good account manager can often uncover in discussions with a buyer—it can also be your ticket to getting more peg hooks devoted to your product line on a crowded retail shelf.

"In my company today, we deal with a real giant—Kraft," Striano told me. He had since moved to dessert vendor Kozy Shack. "Our big competitor is Jell-O in the pudding business. Here we are, a privately held, much smaller company going up against one of the largest food companies in the world—beyond this, one with a brand name. We've been able to carve out a 30 percent share of market that should be dominated completely by such a large company." Kozy Shack has done this with a two-pronged strategy based on a compelling consumer message that resonates with the buying public and the careful management of their inventory—and its subsequent ROII—at the channel level.

Kozy Shack is an all-natural product and the competition is not. "Read their label and it's a chemistry set," Striano explained. "Read ours and there's typically five or six ingredients, most of which you can get out of a kitchen cabinet." This impacts not only consumer perception but also channel inventory management. An all-natural product with no preservatives needs to be refrigerated. This means both manufacturer and retailer need to cooperate to ensure that the product is moving off the shelves promptly to avoid spoilage.

When we look to the comparative ROII calculations of Kozy Shack's dessert products compared to its larger competitor, Jell-O, we see where Striano's competitive strategy pays off. Where ROII is calculated as mark-up multiplied by the inventory turnover, or the number of times a fully stocked retailer sells out of inventory over the course of a year, Kozy Shack's inventory turnover is significantly faster than Jell-O's. This faster turn rate is attributed first to the strong consumer demand for the brand's products as well as the fact that the brand has less inventory per storefront. Remember, the spoilage issue comes into play here, because neither buyer nor seller wants to deal with significant levels of bad inventory on the shelf. As a result, the close cooperation between the two parties ensures that just enough product is stocked in the stores at any given time so that it will sell out with time to spare before spoilage becomes an issue. And if you have fewer slots devoted to your product at the same sales rate, your inventory turnover will be higher: High demand with less inventory per storefront means a need to restock faster—and a higher ROII. Thus, even with comparable margins on both products, Kozy Shack wins the battle for ROII, ensuring its survival on the shelf and spurring periodic evaluation for additional facings. "We typically have a much higher ROII than our competitor does. Our ROII and our all-natural value add spell a very profitable business if it's managed well at retail."

For a channel-based business, managing your ROII effectively is the means to getting yourself in and on the retail planogram. What can a careful reader learn from Kozy Shack, and how can the idea of return on inventory investment be applied?

- **RETURN ON INVENTORY INVESTMENT—ROII, OR GMROI, IF YOU'RE SPEAKING TO WALMART—IS CALCULATED THIS WAY:**

    ROII = [mark-up x inventory turnover].

- **KNOW YOUR ENEMY'S TURNS.** If you understand how fast your inventory turns at retail versus your competitor, you can adjust your margins to deliver a superior ROII calculation. If your giant chooses to reduce their prices to meet you, that's a game they'll have to play over a larger base of business for a prolonged period of time.

- **KNOW YOUR ENEMY'S MARGINS.** If you know the comparative margins between your brand and your giant, you can still deliver a superior ROII by increasing your inventory turns. Your turns will be a function of the amount of inventory your retailer carries—the number of facings they have on the shelf plus inventory—and the speed at which consumers pull them off those shelves and put them in their shopping baskets. Ads, temporary price decreases, displays, value added promotions, and other means of driving demand—not to mention stronger brand loyalty in general—will all, in aggregate, improve your turns.

ROII tells your channel partner how much money they are making on each dollar invested in your inventory every year. In sophisticated retail environments where you're selling an inventoried product, this is the calculation you'll use to get in and get more—at the giant's expense.

Moving Consumers from the Rational to the Emotional: JetBlue's Strategy of Easy Sampling to Create Customer Loyalty

There was a lot of controversy within the company as to whether this promotion was a good idea or not. All the leaders in commercial sat down and gave our predictions as to how many we thought we'd sell. We actually had a pool. So we announced the promotion on a Wednesday morning with a press release and a Tweet. That's it. The final number we sold was actually higher than anyone guessed. None of us guessed we'd sell as many as we sold.

—MARTY ST. GEORGE, SENIOR VICE PRESIDENT OF MARKETING AND COMMERCIAL STRATEGY, JETBLUE

JetBlue talks a lot about bringing humanity back to air travel, but beyond the marketing language that is an obligatory part of every corporate environment, the company is steeped in a set of values that extends from the board room to the terminal. "Everybody knows them, everybody lives them," senior vice president of marketing and commercial strategy Marty St. George explained to me. "You will sit in internal meetings at the most senior levels and we'll debate how a decision might impact the values. Every crewmember knows the five values— safety, caring, integrity, fun, and passion. They can recite them off the top of their heads." Culture at JetBlue, in other words, goes beyond the poster in the break room.

JetBlue's confidence in their ability to deliver a better experience to air travelers comes from their routinely higher load capacity rates—the percentage of their seats that are filled on a monthly basis. And with a product worth bragging about, the company is aggressive about introducing the experience to as many people as it can. "The cheapest marketing tool we have is an empty seat. We can't make money doing that in the long term, but what we think we can do is make new customers who will come back again. The strategy from the very beginning is to sell the seats first. Get people hooked on the experience." Pricing, therefore, is a very strategic competitive weapon, driving the company's weekly promotions—the $9, $19, $29 fares that give those air travelers sitting on the fence that final push to try JetBlue for the first time. "If we were a brand that didn't pull people back, this would be a lousy strategy. We love doing things that customers would say, 'I can't imagine anyone doing this except for JetBlue,' like our $31 fares on Halloween."

A vivid example of how JetBlue samples its experience is its All You Can Jet Pass promotion, the $599 all-access pass that the company first offered in September 2009, giving customers unlimited flights for thirty days. While at first glance, you'd assume this would be an expensive and risky move, even in a risk-tolerant culture, it turns out that the promotion was a calculated bet with little downside. September is JetBlue's worst month for load capacity. The company anticipated having empty seats during this time period, and knowing that the marginal cost of flying one more customer on a flight that was going to take off anyway was minimal, filling these seats in creative ways—preferably with flyers who had yet to experience JetBlue's level of service—was smart and on strategy. Further, the JetBlue team surmised that the offer would only be bought by those travelers who planned on flying more than three times during that thirty-day promotional period. As it turned out, St. George not only landed many of the customers he planned on getting, but many more as well.

From its relatively quiet launch, the $599 pass quickly found its way around social networking sites. Where airline watchers quickly dismissed the promotion as an offer that would only appeal to students and retirees, the idea of an unlimited air pass captured the imagination of a broad spectrum of travelers from all walks of life. Many customers got together on their own to discuss what they planned to do with their month of traveling, using social sites like MeetUp.com to arrange spontaneous get-togethers in local areas. The stories these travelers told quickly dispelled any preconceptions of a narrow appeal. "There was one couple that lived in Austin, but the wife was starting a job in New York, so the husband quit his job a month early and they traveled around for a month," St. George explained, telling me of the first of many of his interactions with pass holders. "A few dot-com entrepreneurs used it as part of their marketing plans. This one guy had three meetings in three cities budgeted in his marketing plan, but with the pass he ended up visiting twenty-five cities. We had a band buy passes and fly around the country doing gigs. We realized this was a bigger deal than we thought it was."

JetBlue's $599 pass was very successful in filling the usually empty seats during their seasonally lightest period and delivered strongly on their goal of bringing in new customers. Importantly, though, it also delivered an avalanche of positive exposure for the JetBlue brand. "The amount of free media impressions we got from this was far bigger than anything we've ever seen," St. George explained. "We actually got significantly more media attention from this promotion than we got from the operational meltdown we had in 2007. This was bigger in the press, media, and blogosphere."

JetBlue's All You Can Jet Pass did more than just fill seats in a clever way. It delivered on JetBlue's mission and values. "We had a contest after the promotion," St. George told me, "which was 'Tell us your story.' We had two categories, one being, 'How did the pass change your life?' and the other being, 'How did the pass change someone else's life?' The stories were incredible. One was a descendent of Frederick Douglass who traveled around talking to elementary schools. We're such a values-based culture—this was a very emotional thing for us. We do not look at this business as a utility. We look at this as bringing people together. Of empowering humanity."

JetBlue's use of pricing as a competitive weapon is an emotional strategy that seeks to share its passion about bringing humanity back to air travel. What lessons can we take away from JetBlue?

- **IF DOGS DON'T LIKE YOUR DOG FOOD, THE PACKAGING DOESN'T MATTER.** If you flew someone else a dozen times in a month, would you still want to fly them? JetBlue and the $599 All You Can Jet Pass are means to a very important end. JetBlue wants you to intensively fly their airline for a month because they believe the experience will turn you into a raving evangelist for the brand. If the experience of flying JetBlue wasn't this good, the promotion would be a disaster.

- **PRICING IS MARKETING, AND YOU CAN'T SEPARATE MARKETING FROM CULTURE FOR VERY LONG.** When St. George says he wants customers to say, "I could only imagine this coming from JetBlue," he is telling us something very important. In a landscape littered with me-too offers, St. George is proud to offer promotions that are individual branding statements. He strives to make each offer unique to his brand.

- **WHAT'S VIVID IS REMEMBERED LONG AFTER WHAT'S VALID IS FORGOTTEN.** Or, in the words of Duke Ellington, "It don't mean a thing if it ain't got that swing." Offering up a $599 All You Can Jet Pass for a month, the moral equivalent of the Eurail pass, grabbed attention. People had never seen anything like this coming from an airline. Could the careful air traveler have compared prices and cobbled together an itinerary that was cheaper than JetBlue's? Probably, depending on how many stops they planned to make. But that's the whole point. You read about this sort of offer and you're swept up in what it could mean to you, personally. You—along with everyone else at your local "meet-up"—become emotionally committed

129

to the idea. The price becomes a different factor. Your emotional polarity has been flipped from rational to emotional.

JetBlue provides us with a clear example of pricing as an extension of both brand and strategy, where the offer is as unique as their fingerprint and serves to accomplish the brand's single most important mission: to create evangelists.

Moving Consumers from Emotional to Rational: Zipcar and Consumption Without Ownership

The big idea is changing cars from products into services. People can get access to a car as easily and as affordably as they could by owning it by using our service. I think that's a big idea.

—SCOTT GRIFFITH, CEO OF ZIPCAR

What does your car cost you on an hourly basis? If you're like most U.S. car owners, you spend an average of $700 a month on car payments, insurance, gas, and all the other bits and pieces that together create the car ownership experience. And, if you're like most drivers in the United States, you drive your car roughly one hour per day. That works out to $23 per hour of use. But you can't own your car by the hour. You sign up for the whole $700 per month and you get what you get for it.

Your alternative, in a growing number of cities in the United States and the UK, is to join Zipcar's growing ranks of members, and get wheels when you want them for as low as $8 per hour—including gas and insurance. Zipcar promises all the benefits of wheels when you want them without the hassle of actually owning a car.

Zipcar sells memberships that allow its customers—its Zipsters—to rent its fleet of cars with an all-inclusive price on an hourly basis. There are no surprises that typify traditional car rentals: gas and insurance are included, for example. The cars themselves are distributed in small "pods" throughout the cities where the company is currently available, so its customers no longer have to trek to the outskirts near the airport to pick up a car. For urban dwellers and others with modest transportation needs, the ability to have access to an automobile as easily as one might rent a DVD is not only convenient but economically practical as well.

"The average U.S. household spends 19 percent on transportation, whereas the average Zipster spends 6 percent," Scott Griffith told me. "This value is magnified during times of economic stress, or other variables like high gas prices. We grew 70 percent in 2009, during the worst recession of our lives. We're building a lasting, trusted relationship with our members. Zipsters are making a smart choice that helps them save money, live a more sustainable lifestyle, and do some good for their community, too. That's powerful."

The company and its user base have traveled a long way since the company's launch in 2003. "Our initial customers were urban dwellers who occasionally need cars but didn't want to own one," Griffith told me. Today, Zipsters are increasingly realizing that personal transportation doesn't necessarily mean they need to buy a car. "When they do that math, it just doesn't pencil for some people who want that lifestyle. They can run errands, go to the beach, visit friends . . . they don't want to give that up, but they want to do it in the most affordable, smart way. They're thinking about the impact of the choices they make around consumption. It's still a pretty fresh trend, it's pretty new. Between affordability and smart lifestyle choices and externalities, I think there's an emerging class of consumers who are much more tuned in to this than there ever were before."

The suggestion that membership-based personal transportation might be going mainstream may strike one as a bit premature until we step back and look at the forces at play, both within the nascent car-sharing industry and taking the vast sweep of social and technological change into consideration as well. First, look at the growing array of products available through fractional ownership, from software as a service (SaaS) to high fashion, vacation homes, DVDs, and books. Beyond this growing ubiquity of choice, we see the very real constraints of physical urban space available for parking cars together with the growing desire to curb emissions, both from the public sector as well as from consumers themselves. A large percentage of Zipcar's current clientele is realizing that one of life's biggest investments—buying a car—isn't necessarily an expense they have to plan for anymore. Once we recognize that smart phones and services delivered by the Internet and leveraging location-based technology are ubiquitous, many of the purchasing choices we once considered the "givens" of modern life can be swept aside.

This trend we'll call "smart consumerism" may be the most powerful force driving Zipcar's growth. "I believe there's a fine line between being frugal and being a smart consumer," Griffith related. "Frugality implies going without, or sacrificing. Smart consumerism is about getting what you want, but at a lower price, more conveniently, or getting more value. People still want high quality, but they want value more than ever. We like to think of our members as the original smart consumers. After all, we've been around for a decade, and have seen both the go-go days of the mid-2000s and now the recession. Through both eras, smart consumers have realized they can reduce hassle and save money with Zipcar. We think this is an enduring phenomenon."

With the company announcing its plans for an IPO in June 2010, where does it go from here? "We envision a world where there are more car sharers than car owners in major cities around the world, and that Zipcar can be a major contributor to enabling simple, responsible urban living."

Zipcar provides an example of how one brand can change the face of an iconic consumer relationship—in this case, owning a car. What enduring lessons can we take away from Zipcar?

- **ACKNOWLEDGE THE RISE OF SMART CONSUMERISM.** The Great Recession of 2008 to 2009 taught us all a painful lesson. We still want a high degree of quality and convenience, but we want it at a lower cost of ownership. Brands that can find creative ways to do this will get a second look.

- **REIMAGINE OWNERSHIP.** Owning a car has been part of the "American Dream" since the turn of the century before this one. Our relationships with our cars are part of our cultural roots. Turning this idea on its head and offering transportation not as a product but as a service was a solution hidden in plain sight. There are always other ways to offer your product or service—and owning it outright might not be the best choice for everyone.

- **HOW MANY PEOPLE LIKE FINE PRINT?** Zipcar's all-inclusive pricing jabs a questioning finger in the open wound of the car rental world and reminds us to always wonder aloud who is in the most pain. Car rental companies, infamous for their fine print for so long, are now scrambling to catch up in a category once considered their sole preserve. When we ask ourselves, "Who is dissatisfied with the status quo?" we often find ourselves looking at industries and opportunities that have been givens for a long time.

- **FROM SIMPLE ECONOMICS TO LIFESTYLES AND RELATIONSHIPS.** Zipcar's basic economics originally appealed to a small set of hand-raisers in urban environments, but as the company gained traction, a new set of consumers emerged, some possibly pushed by macroeconomic forces, that simply gravitated to the brand. From humble beginnings that promised a lighter environmental footprint at a lower cost emerged a friendly brand that simply made more sense.

- **TIMING AND MARKET MATURITY PLAY A BIG ROLE.** Zipcar wouldn't have been possible if consumers didn't have smart phones or mobile Web technologies at their fingertips, nor would it have been an easy jump if consumers hadn't already trained themselves on Internet sharing services like Netflix. There would have been too many new "news" in the mix. Zipcar took advantage of a number of groundswell ideas, technologies, and attitudes and launched a service where once there was only a product.

Zipcar serves as a valuable lesson for anyone looking at reimagining an established industry with a novel pricing model—in this case, taking what is often a fairly large capital expense and turning it into an affordable membership.

Key Takeaways

Smart brands wield **Inconvenient Truths** like slingshots for toppling giants. What key takeaways can we extract from these companies?

Move your customer from the emotional to the rational. How can you flip the emotional polarity of your customers from purely emotional thinking to a normal functioning state where they can understand what's in their best interests? There's always room to introduce your customers to new ways of doing what they've always done, especially if you're a structural game-changer like Zipcar. America has always had a love affair with its cars, and Zipcar is convincing them in increasing numbers that personal transportation doesn't have to equal product ownership. Do the math. Does it make more sense to get your wheels when you need them?

Winning the ROII game versus a giant is a balancing act. For a channel-based business where inventory turns and markups determine profitability, managing ROII is how you get in and grow. Get the competitive data. Do the math. Understand where you fall in the comparative analysis and do what you need to do to make a better financial decision than your giant for those scarce dollars your buyer has to devote to your category. When faced with a competitor with greater customer sell-through, understand the math and make up for it in margin. When dealing with a competitor with more margin, do everything possible to punch up your sell-through.

Understand the short-term tools you have at your disposal that can juice your sell-through. Co-op advertising, all manner of off-planogram displays and temporary price decreases— plus combinations of all three—can dial up your sell-through this quarter, and sometimes even this month. Your judicious use of value-added promotional overlays and consumer promotion, your judicious use of retail detailers to do demo days, and other in-store activities and other longer-term consumer pull activities all impact your sell-through and thus your ROII.

Move your customers from the rational to the emotional. How can you persuade a customer who knows they're getting a "good deal from a respectable brand" to drop the product they're holding like a forgotten toy and rush to your offer? Give them something to get excited about. All You Can Jet for $599? For a whole month? That gets people's attention. It taps more than just the "rational mind-set" and casts us back to our days backpacking across Europe with our Eurail pass and our phrasebook. What adventures could I have with a month of unlimited travel?

We've moved people away from the purely rational and tapped something more fundamental.

Firsthand experience is often the best teacher. If the incremental cost of adding one more customer is close to zero—and your experience is word-of-mouth-worthy—why wouldn't you want everyone to sample your product? "Free"—or even "close to free"—is a powerful price point. By offering a product for little to nothing, you let everyone sample your experience. If you're good, they'll come back. If you're great, they'll tell all their friends, and blog about it to boot.

When your market is in pain, make it easy to switch. We don't trust brands very much anymore and it's the fault of every brand marketer who has helped perpetuate an atmosphere of overpromising and underdelivering. Zipcar's Scott Griffith tells us that "a number of industries have created this monster of distrust. The airlines charge you for a pillow and a blanket, for crying out loud. Brands are being built on one transaction at a time where people can search your brand experience in real time." Paul Leinberger of The Futures Company tells us, "We're looking for companies that are working as hard as we are. Don't tell me you feel my pain, because we don't believe that garbage. If you make mistakes, own up to them and I will recognize it for what it is, but somehow I need to believe you're on my side. I need you to be fair."

So if the giant's dog food irritates the hell out of your market's dogs, make it easy to switch. How many "gotchas" does the average car rental company sting you with? Why do I have to pay double for gas if I don't fill it back up? Zipcar gives us a very reasonable alternative without the eye-rolling problems. Instead of playing the usual game, Zipcar changes the entire equation of what it takes to drive when and where you want—and for how much.

How can you change the shape of the transaction to make the sale in a more palatable way? Challenge the givens. When you need a hole, that doesn't mean you necessarily have to buy a drill, do you? You just need a hole. That's all. You can certainly make a hole with a drill. You can also make a hole with a screwdriver, a hammer, your fist, a gun, or a number of other handy items. Someone shopping for a car is really shopping for personal transportation, aren't they? They don't necessarily need to buy a car to drive one from here to there whenever they need it. And for those with pocket problems, the significantly lower cost of "usership" makes a lot of sense. Change the shape of the transaction. From "bottom of the pyramid" examples of single-serving-size packets of detergent to the fractional ownership model for luxury executive jets, changing the shape of the transaction changes our expectations and lowers the barriers to acceptance.

CHAPTER SEVEN: *Polarize on Purpose*

You're not like everybody else. You don't even try to fit in. And that's OK. You create meaningful separation from the other alternatives in the market and force your customer to make a very specific choice. You and your giant are very different animals—something you've worked hard to make clear—and you thrive by drawing attention to your differences.

No one chooses you by accident. Force the decision. They're either with you or against you. Polarize your market on purpose.

Stories are distillations of life . . . we abstract from life, we copy from life, we create something that looks as if it were life, but what we create is far more powerful and meaningful. Artists have insights into life and a way of distilling it down to what is essential.

—ROBERT McKEE, SCREENWRITER, AUTHOR, AND TEACHER

We're all in the business of storytelling. Regardless of whether you're a writer grinding out your first screenplay or a CEO breathing new life into the vision she presents to a skeptical board, you need to capture your audience's imagination.

Why is this important? Because to persuade others, you need them on your side. And when you tell someone a story, they instinctively want things to work out for the protagonist—who, in this case, happens to be you.

If we're all students of story, Robert McKee is our most respected and quoted teacher. McKee's Story Seminar has been attended by more than fifty thousand students, who in total have produced screenplays that have won 29 Academy Awards, more than 160 Emmy Awards, 21 Writers Guild of America Awards, and 17 Directors Guild of America Awards, among other accomplishments. The three-day, thirty-hour seminar is a fire hose of insight into the structure and nuance of story development, even if your instrument of choice happens to be PowerPoint and the biggest screen you ever aspire to appear on is lowered in front of a conference room wall.

Why do stories matter in a life of business? Why do we need to dramatize real-life facts and data? Isn't telling the truth enough? It is, but stories *are* "true"—they are distillations of human experience. "The whole process of telling a story is to crack open the gap in reality between what a character expects to happen when they take an action and what actually does when they do," McKee told me. "In that moment of surprise there's an insight into the character, into their history, into society, which has been prepared by the writer . . . it's been planted previously. It went by with the first meaning and it made perfect sense. But in that turning point, it sends the audience back to discover the meaning that's underneath it. The second meaning is far deeper and far more important. The first may look somewhat trivial, but the second expresses how and why what just happened, happened, in a deeper, more powerful and broader manner, and with more gravity and importance that what you thought it did."

In that moment of surprise, these revealed insights into

our characters reveal the choices they've made under pressure. When faced with danger, we react without great deliberation—and these reactions speak volumes about who we fundamentally are, not who we'd like others to think we are. This distillation of human experience that we experience when we're hearing the story—with all its faults, flaws, and eccentricities—is what we respond to, regardless of whether we're talking about a person or a brand.

Stories are important to a life of business because they are not exaggerations or caricatures of life but distillations of life. We respond to stories because they help us make sense of the world. As critic Edmund Burke said, "Stories are equipment for living."

WHAT SEPARATES TRULY UNIQUE BRANDS—as opposed to just "different" ones—is that, like our protagonist (you), they push us to make choices. How do we as stewards of brands achieve meaningful separation in the eyes of our public? How do we put enough daylight between our brand and our giant competitors so that a consumer can truly see us for who we are?

This isn't a question of being different for the sake of being different. Differentiation without discipline is self-indulgence. Many successful brands that have achieved separation have done so because they have avoided becoming exaggerations of what makes them different and have distilled the meaning that these points of difference make to us on an emotional level.

This distillation process has profound implications for how we approach positioning our differences. We're subtractive, not additive. Caricatures layer more on top of more—more ideas, more angles, more things to more people. Over time, the caricature brand tends to mean lots of different things and ultimately stands for nothing.

To combat this insidious feature-creep of brand addition,

we can study those brands that have successfully put meaningful separation between themselves and the giants they face by chipping away at the nonessentials. These are brands that are distilled and refined, that have polarized their markets intentionally and strategically.

What do our consumers get out of all of this introspection on our part? Lots, as it turns out. By making this polarizing choice of choosing a brand that is both unique and utterly authentic, they do more than just pick a product—they separate themselves from the herd as well. Our choice defines us, at least for those brief moments every day when we become conscious of the product and the implications of our choice. We briefly give our consumers a point of view, a sense of identity that they can tap into that also creates, when done skillfully, a sense of community and exclusivity.

Drawing Attention to Impossible Smallness: MINI USA

They're driving like there is a tomorrow.

—JIM McDOWELL, GM OF MINI USA

Standing apart in an American automotive landscape long dominated by cars the size of city blocks, there's MINI. The MINI brand has evolved from its impossibly small roots into a complex but still personal statement of values, stewardship, community, and fun.

"We view ourselves as a culture and a community," VP and general manager Jim McDowell told me. "MINI knows that we are an impossibly small car for most Americans. But there are a small number of people that want a car that is a personal decision. MINI is a performance car in a remarkably compact package that can be customized to reflect you, your driving needs, your personality. We knew it was a proposition that wouldn't appeal to 95 percent of the population, but for that 5 percent of the population, this was the absolute perfect choice."

Listen to what McDowell says here. MINI isn't for everyone. It's *impossibly small*. But for a small group of hand-raisers, it's a perfect choice. And the choice this relatively small group makes when they buy a MINI separates them from the herd of SUV drivers who dominate the other 95 percent of the market.

But within this exclusive group, there's a sense of inclusion, of group identity. "We're inclusive as a community for people that in many ways are post-material. They're self-actualizing people, they're making purchase decisions that are right for them, not for their neighbors. They're not buying status symbols. They're also very much aware of the fact that they're not gobbling up all the world's resources by driving a MINI."

This idea of exclusivity takes on greater meaning when we understand that the brand's option package is so vast that there are more than 15 trillion potential combinations. In a world increasingly defined by simplification of choice, MINI offers personalization taken to an extreme.

MINI's efforts to polarize its market don't stop here. Not only is your MINI likely to be the only one of its kind on the road, you'll find the "Eccentricities of your MINI" quick-start guide in your new car, giving you an insider's look at all the features a non-MINI owner has never seen before, from the saucer-size mid-dashboard speedometer and the right-hand-side bonnet release—both nods to the brand's British and auto rally heritage—to the "openometer" meter that records the amount of time your convertible's bonnet has been open.

Look at how the brand has animated its position to consumers. At launch, the MINI On Top campaign paraded the car—comfortably perched atop a Ford Expedition—through several major metro areas, with a billboard reading: "What are you doing for fun this weekend?" Marketing manager Trudy Hardy explained, "The fun stuff goes up on top of your car for the weekend. It also showed how absurdly large some of these SUVs really are." A rolling, vivid example of the contrast principle: a massive American SUV with a MINI on top, the moral equivalent of a bike or a kayak, poised for a big weekend of fun.

Look at the brand's product integration in both the original 1969 version and the 2003 remake of the film *The Italian Job.* Both feature exciting chase scenes that hinge upon doing what only a MINI can do—navigating through tight spaces, eluding bad guys on crowded streets, and, in both films, driving through sewer tunnels. "For most people in the U.S. who didn't see the original *Italian Job*, it was their first exposure to the car," Hardy told me. "It had a huge impact, and people to this day still say it is what they remember most about MINI. Our dealers stated that the traffic coming into the stores during that time period was largely due to the movie and the awareness it created for our new brand." An impossibly small car, a performance car in a compact package, presented in an aspirational setting, doing things only a very small car with high performance could possibly do. This is as perfect a product placement as you're going to get—and it set the brand, and the car, like a jewel in the minds of the buying public.

Let's review MINI against the metaphor of poker—Texas hold 'em—to animate the point. What is obvious—our face-up card—is the brand's distinctive size. The car is a scant twelve feet long. Small can still mean small. But going beyond the obvious, we see the hidden value—the hole card, facedown, visible only to us on our side of the table: Small means less space on the road, leaving more space for everyone. MINI embodies a smaller footprint not only on the street but on the environment. Being "impossibly small" may mean toylike to the cynical, but the team at MINI USA fully embraces this idea and pushes it further to include the idea of play, fun, and joy.

What enduring lessons can we take away from MINI?

- **MINI'S "IMPOSSIBLE SMALLNESS" IS THE OBVIOUS PHYSICAL TRAIT, BUT THE BRAND'S POLARIZING NATURE IS DEFINED BY WHAT "MINI" REALLY MEANS:** community, fun, joy, minimalist, post-big, post-materialist, independent, aware, courteous, responsible.

- **IT ISN'T ENOUGH TO BE DIFFERENT.** You need to reinforce how different you are. The "Eccentricities of Your MINI" card, the MINI On Top campaign, and other factors don't stop at the car's physical size.

- **EXCLUSIVITY BREEDS COMMUNITY.** Shared experience and publicly stated positions reinforce behaviors. We all feel tremendous personal and interpersonal pressure to behave in a manner consistent with our previously stated positions. MINI builds upon this to foster a greater sense of community and brand loyalty.

MINI is a study in giving your audience the opportunity to choose a different path, one with meaningful separation from the road more commonly traveled, and reinforcing your new customer's decision along the way.

Reimagining the Overnight Stay: Prizeotel

Our problem is that people don't always realize we're a budget product. They think it's a four-star product, but we're a two-star product at a two-star price.

—MARCO NUSSBAUM, CEO AND COFOUNDER OF PRIZEOTEL

Prizeotel is a contradiction. "We are a design hotel, designed by an international designer, but we're a budget product," CEO and Prizeotel founder Marco Nussbaum explained. "We are a signature brand hotel—the whole hotel is designed by Karim Rashid—the furniture, the bed, the walls, everything. Others will put a designer chair in the lobby and call themselves a design hotel. This is the cutting edge that gives us the advantage over everybody."

The idea that good design is akin to a human right is a central belief in internationally renowned designer Karim Rashid's philosophy. "Good design should exist everywhere," he explains. "I slept in over a hundred hotels last year and have come across every bad design, nuisance, and irritation in the hotel industry. I've knocked over unstable tables, had an impossible time finding light switches, been forced to stare at an ill-placed ceiling utility grill . . . hotels, whether high- or low-end, boutique or super-chain, should serve the human needs of the guests."

To fully understand what makes Prizeotel work, let's take a quick look at the mechanics of how a budget hotel business operates. The first requirement is low labor cost, so the hotel's processes were designed to save time, effort, and money without dramatically impacting the experience. Nonessential features were the first ones to go: If you want a drink, you go to the lobby bar and buy one to take back to your room. This means no mini-bars—or the labor costs associated with restocking them. With every business traveler carrying a mobile phone today, why do we need a landline phone in the room? Removing these eliminated the cost of the terminals and the infrastructure needed to support them. Gone, too, are the pay TV channels, along with the customer service labor costs needed to debate whether a movie was watched or not. By eliminating those charges that normally occur after a guest checks in, Prizeotel simply charges for the room in total when the guest checks in. When the guest checks out, there's no checkout line, no wait, no hassle—and no need to staff the desk for checkout in the morning, either.

Apart from streamlining the hotel's processes, the physical design involved constant trade-offs between costs and performance. "The design had to be very smart, to maximize choices and use materials to have maximum impact," Rashid explained. "The budget constraints were challenging, but we were able to find solutions and suppliers that provided high design for little cost." Large windows allow natural light to come into the bathroom area, giving the impression of more space. Saving on closet space was another innovation. "The average stay in a hotel is 1.2 days, and therefore guests travel with little in the way of luggage," Rashid explained. "So we provided a closet in the bedrooms where guests were staying more than two nights, and in the other 50 percent of the rooms we put a bench with a small hanging space. This provided considerable savings."

But for all the things one doesn't see, a guest also experiences subtle touches that contradict the hotel's modest price tag. An iPod player integrated into a lamp, a flat-screen TV, a glass closet door (for those with closets), a custom light sculpture, and free WiFi aren't features you'd expect in a room with a fifty-nine euro price tag. And Prizeotel is renovated every six months, so unlike many of its competitors, it never looks dilapidated.

Does this idea work with paying customers? "The hotel has the highest occupancy in Bremen," Nussbaum explained. "The average occupancy of a good hotel in Germany today is 60 percent. Bremen is a little lower. We will end the year at about 85 percent. We tried to achieve being the leading design and economy hotel. What we've achieved in Bremen is to become number one on the review sites."

What enduring lessons can we take away from Prizeotel?

- **QUESTION THE GIVENS.** Prizeotel is an exercise in questioning the prevailing wisdom of what constitutes a budget hotel and making decisions that at first may appear strange.

- **A SUPERIOR PRODUCT IS BUILT FROM ITS CONSTRAINTS, NOT ITS FEATURES.** Prizeotel, on paper, shouldn't work: a signature design hotel that fits within the budget segment. The idea that you can design a product based on seemingly incompatible constraints should be inspirational to anyone.

- **APPLY RIGOROUS DISCIPLINE TO WHAT IS NECESSARY, WHAT IS IMPORTANT, AND WHAT CAN GO.** Designing around constraints is an exercise in making intelligent trade-offs. How often do we see landline telephones in hotel rooms? Do we ever question why they're there when we all carry mobile phones? What was the likely reaction in the room when this was first discussed?

- **DESIGN THINKING ALWAYS MATTERS.** Creating a better customer experience, regardless of your product category, can make up for many shortcomings. A budget hotel is supposed to be Spartan in its atmosphere, so the experience of staying in a room with carefully thought-out design elements is unexpected and welcome. When the superior customer experience is positioned as an additional gift—after all, you're saving money by staying in a budget hotel—and not as the rationale for a significantly higher price, it's a serious competitive advantage.

Prizeotel shows us that you can design a product that defies convention, combining seemingly incompatible extremes of low price, high design, and customer experience by approaching physical, process, and experience design with extreme discipline.

The "Lovable Rogue," Viral Fandom, and Controversy: 42Below

We needed an advantage—our competitors could outspend and out-muscle us at distribution. But they also tended to be a little boring and slow. So our way in was to be faster, with a harder edge that bartenders and drinkers would gravitate to.

—GEOFF ROSS, FOUNDER OF 42BELOW VODKA

42Below is an unapologetic brand. For a product category defined more often by the bottle than by the beverage itself, 42Below vodka is known by its devoted fans as not only a super-premium, award-winning spirit, but a quintessential example of New Zealand brashness, of political incorrectness, and of irreverence bordering on psychosis. To many seasoned PR professionals, a brief tour of 42Below's communications legacy would reduce them to tears. One would think that brands shouldn't do what 42Below did. But that's the point. Geoff Ross distilled a brand in his garage that was as clear in its strategy as its bottles are on the shelf. And it wasn't for everybody.

"The brand is committed to irreverence." Simon Young is the principal of sy, a New Zealand digital marketing agency. "42Below is about confidence and controversy. And they've got a founder who's comfortable with publicity." Ross concurs, to a degree. "People are so jaded with corporate blandness. They

149

love the irreverence and the honesty that a little lovable rogue like New Zealand can exhibit." Irreverence was never the starting point, though. "We set out to do the things our competitors couldn't," Ross said. "We needed an advantage—our competitors could outspend and out-muscle us at distribution. But they also tended to be a little boring and slow. And bartenders thought this. So our way in was to be faster, with a harder edge that bartenders and drinkers would gravitate to. That was the thinking that would start it off for us."

The 42Below brand—so named for its home country's latitude—was the product of creativity meeting frustration. "I was kind of getting a bit dissatisfied giving my ideas to others," Ross explained, referring to his previous life at ad agency Saatchi & Saatchi. "I was sick of great ideas being killed off by bureaucracy or because they were too edgy or risky. Rather than get twisted about it, I thought I should put my money where my mouth is and create my own brand." He continued: "From the start I wanted to do things differently—do them in a way that would get people talking about us. Because we were smaller than the major liquor groups, we needed to do stuff that stands out. Taking risks actually works to our advantage."

42Below is built upon two fundamental pillars. First, consider the company's attention to product quality, from its long list of international awards—the brand touts itself as being "the world's most awarded vodka"—to its use of bottles made half a world away in France. The second is its deliberately unapologetic attitude. "A lot of people said you can't have a brand that is both luxury and irreverent," Ross said. "We disagreed."

While the product quality came from what Ross described as his insistence on identifying the brand with New Zealand's natural and pristine image, he gives much of the credit for the brand's edgy tone to agency colleague Darryl Parsons. "Darryl convinced me that the brand can be luxury and super premium and irreverent at the same time. That stood us apart from many of the other 'serious' vodkas out there. Being non-PC became something drinkers respected us for."

But if 42Below relied on strong brand tension internally, the tension really came out in its advertising. One early online video campaign managed to squeeze in all known New Zealand stereotypes, from sheep and America's Cup yachts to the All Blacks football team, concluding with Maori tribesmen trading their handcrafted vodka with the white man for blankets, muskets, and hobbits. Other videos poked fun at the Germans for having nothing but efficient public transportation, the French for their outsized opinion of their global political importance, and even the Canadians for believing that New Zealand is part of Australia.

Perhaps the brand's most notorious video was aimed at the gay market—"the pink dollar," as it was described—which ran through the entire catalog of gay stereotypes. The video wasn't universally loved by the gay community, needless to say, which threatened a boycott.

"My view is that brands are like people," Ross told me. "You would far rather spend time with a person that is many things . . . clever, witty, is sound and dependable, a joker . . . this is in contrast to a lot of old brand thinking that states a brand should only be one thing."

Bacardi was attracted to 42Below's New Zealandishness enough to purchase the brand in 2006. Bacardi New Zealand's managing director, Paul Dibbayawan, told me, "42Below's culture, sales approach, and marketing all appealed to us . . . an overused term is being entrepreneurial, but breaking this down to its simplest form, the founders of 42Below were creative in every aspect and did not let obstacles—whether financial, social, or regulatory—slow them down."

Since the acquisition, Bacardi has committed to keeping most of the core elements that made 42Below unique, namely the culture and its marketing. Clearly, the new parents will be challenged in trying to keep this upstart brand within its internal tolerances for edginess while retaining all the things that made the brand attractive to them in the first place. What enduring lessons can we learn from 42Below?

- **WHEN YOU DECIDE TO BE "EDGY," UNDERSTAND THAT YOU'RE EDGY TO THE END.** This is not a strategy for the faint of heart. This is not something one casually reverses when the chairman's wife gets uncomfortable, nor is it a "cool idea" from a dude in marketing. As a matter of fact, being edgy as a core brand attribute is a matter of DNA and not a decision made in a conference room. Things will get ugly. And you won't back down.

- **DECIDE WHO YOU'RE NOT.** Polarizing your market for a reason means you accept the fact that not everyone is going to sing along with you. Some will be put off by what you're doing. However, for those who see themselves in what you've created, you will have created a deeper sense of "we" for every fan who's in on the joke and who embraces the humor and the insider feeling of your brand. Instead of being safe and vanilla, you've decided to make a choice and be something more personal to a smaller group of hard-core customers.

- **LET YOUR FANS TELL YOUR STORY.** 42Below relied on the viral nature of their best video work to build their brand with drinkers and bartenders. "The great thing about virals is people vote with their mouse," Ross explained. "If they love it, they pass it on. If they don't, they delete. So we didn't care too much about how right or wrong it was. If people loved one of our virals, it flew. If they didn't like it, they would delete and no more than a few people would see it. But for the drinkers—all they saw is the ones that people loved." Imagine only having your best work be visible to the wider world. Your core audience manages your message for you. This is an important insight for brands with passionate insiders.

- **JUST BEING DIFFERENT IS NOT ENOUGH.** 42Below is a superpremium product that stands among the best of the best in its category from a quality standpoint. If the product didn't work, the branding would have failed. This point of brand tension—of two ideas, never just one standing alone—is an important element of the 42Below story.

42Below shows us an example of a high-quality brand that began with a credible quality story rooted in its unique "New Zealandishness" and then took a decidedly humorous, politically incorrect turn in its branding. This doesn't work for everybody. As a matter of fact, it doesn't usually work at all. For brands flirting with "edginess," 42Below provides a framework for understanding the potential upsides and downsides of a high-risk, high-reward strategy.

Getting Out of Your Own Way:
Indium Corporation

What does a giant have? Money. What am I not spending? Money. They cannot find me in the ring. They can't find me to squash.

—RICK SHORT, MARKETING MANAGER, INDIUM CORPORATION

Electronics materials manufacturers are like a lot of other business-to-business industries. They do booths at trade shows, they run print ads, they wine and dine buyers, they generally do things the way they've always done them. It takes an "emperor has no clothes" moment for the careful observer to stand up and order a full stop on the status quo. For Rick Short, a long-time marketing veteran of Indium Corporation, that moment came when he looked at his customers and the messages his industry was sending them and realized it didn't add up.

"We have extremely sophisticated customers," Short explained, describing the buyers of his company's metals, salts, and solders so common in the manufacturing processes of technology products. "These are master's degree engineers and technologists. There is no opinion. This is all data-driven. No trickery, no tomfoolery will be tolerated." As we all know, tomfoolery is the norm in many industries when it comes to massaging the message. Rick's epiphany came when he recognized that engineering-speak—the thing we so often try to avoid in marketing messaging—is the only language his very particular customers wanted to hear. The industry had somehow put an interpreter in between two people who didn't need the help. "The basic principle of what we're doing at our company is stepping out of the way and letting technologists speak with technologists," Short explained. "We currently have seventy-three blogs authored by fourteen bloggers."

Where transparency has become synonymous with "the CEO just penned his one and only blog post," Indium has become the branding equivalent of crystal glass. Not content to merely let technologists speak directly to customers, Indium has made these engineers and other specialists the face of the company—individually. "If you go to market as one company, you've only got one voice or brand," Short explained. "If you turn your company inside out and expose fifteen technologists and let each of them talk about what and why they're doing what they're doing, you've got fifteen different brands. And you can't tell me that any one company's voice is more interesting than a person's voice. We've multiplied the quantity, but we've multiplied the quality of what we go to market with—real people, real stories, real experience, real passion."

What happens when you unleash a dozen highly specialized technologists with self-publishing tools and a free mandate to write about what they do and how they do it? You shorten the distance between questions and answers, and between inquiries and sales. No more call centers and salespeople calling back later. "Engage with my company and you know exactly who you want to talk to because it's the person you've been following, who's intrigued you, who's earned your trust," Short explained. "What I'm trying to do is convert the predominant volume of my callers from shoppers to people who are on fire. Here's my name, here's my address. You know the problems I'm experiencing because you know that I just downloaded two white papers on this exact subject. Sometimes, when people download a paper, they get a phone call from one of my people and they say, 'Oh my gosh, thanks for calling!' Compare that to a cold call. It's so opt in, so invitation only, and it's so appreciated." Demand generation and lead qualification have just become the same step. The traditional sales funnel has collapsed into a one-step process.

How has this strategy of creating a publishing network of highly skilled technologists worked out for them? Short shared three primary benefits with me. "We freed up a ton of cash because we don't spend money the way we spent money. We now know a more productive way of spending money, and it's wildly less." When you don't rely on above-the-line marketing expense to drive leads into your funnel, you've got more money to do other things. The second insight was one of perception. "We're no longer talking the kind of language that our customers despise—we have enhanced our technological integrity. We go to market with technical data, with the content our customers need to have." Customers now call with the correct white paper in hand, asking for the specific category expert by name. And when Indium sees a particular Web site visitor leaving their contact information and downloading a series of white papers on a particular problem, their call is not only accepted but greatly appreciated. The sales funnel is shorter than it used to be. Last, the change in focus has had an impact internally, on the very people creating the content. "Technologists in our company say they've never been treated like this. 'You truly respect me. You put me up front.' We call these people our rock stars. It's created great morale."

Indium is a company that has turned itself inside out for its customers. They've replaced massive trade show booths and overblown print ad copy with fresh, first-person content from the experts. As a result, they've shortened the time it takes to get from "I have a burning problem" to "I know a materials scientist who can help me." This also means that the distance between "inquiry" and "sale" is similarly shortened. "I provide more compelling content, which becomes more high-quality contacts for my sales team to convert to sales. When you do that at higher volumes and a higher rate using fewer resources . . . if you do that, management won't ask you any other questions."

What enduring lessons can we take away from Indium?

- **WHAT LANGUAGE DOES YOUR CUSTOMER SPEAK?** Find out and speak to them in the language they want to be spoken to in. Speak down to them and they'll oblige you by going elsewhere.

- **RELATIONSHIPS ARE BUILT ON CREDIBILITY, NOT COCKTAILS.** All things being equal, it's good to build relationships with important business contacts. When was the last time that all things were equal? You can build a social relationship based on credibility a lot faster than you can build credibility based on a social relationship.

- **THE FEWER MOVING PARTS, THE BETTER.** Companies that have problems communicating, whether internally or externally, don't need to communicate more. They need to reduce the need to communicate. Connecting those in need with those who provide is the shortest distance between two points.

- **NO ONE SELLS A PEER LIKE A PEER.** No one is as technical as a technical expert. Materials scientists like to speak to other materials scientists. They need to. They demand it. If you think that there's a role for fluffy language and artistic executions, you need to remember that marketing is about understanding the needs of your customer—not winning an Oscar.

- **WHAT DOES YOUR CUSTOMER NEED TO KNOW?** Are they buying on emotion, or scarcity, or out of a sense of reciprocity? Or are they objectively buying on evidence and fact? Know what is essential—dig until you understand the distilled need of your market—and throw out the rest.

- **WHAT DO YOU NEED TO KNOW?** Distill your own internal metrics while you're at it. It's not about buzz, fuzziness, or clicks. It's about sales. The shorter the distance between engagement and sell-through, the better.

There is no fluff in Indium's communications strategy—as a matter of fact, the fluff has been carefully excised in favor of pure content. Indium provides us with a business-to-business story of distilled authenticity, of subject matter experts pushed to the fore to speak directly to those who want to hear what they have to say.

Key Takeaways

Polarize on Purpose discusses how smart brands create meaningful separation from the herd and distill their points of differentiation to their cores. This is a strategy that can work when your brand, product—and, most important, culture—are meaningfully different from those of your giant. But it requires you to strip away the nonessential trappings of your brand and concentrate on the core. What key takeaways can we extract from this lesson?

Understand your "down card." Think of what words you and your customers use to describe your brand. What is your brand's "controlling idea," its distillation? Once you've defined who you are at your core, what does this require you to do? What associations are now possible because of the choices you've made? MINI isn't just "small"—it's fun, it's responsible, and it's community. Prizeotel isn't just "budget"—its speed, convenience, and affordable luxury, a design hotel reimagined for business travelers. Is 42Below just another premium vodka brand? No! It's what's fun and interesting in life, humor and good times. It's for insiders. Indium, too, is anything but one of the good ol' boys in the materials business. They're experts. Period.

Once you've distilled your message, you can draw your hub and extend the spokes outward into just those associations that are believable, credible, and ownable for you and your brand.

Meaningful separation can be attained by doing the impossible, either in form, function, or message. How have you structured your constraints so that you've made meaningful, and often painful, decisions that determine what you are and what you aren't? When you choose to polarize your market, you've made a decision to leave certain things out. "What are the choices we make?" Robert McKee exhorts us. "The rest is just body and fender work."

Polarizing means always having to say you're sorry (to

someone, at least). Who are you willing to draw closer to you—and who are you willing to push away? You're never catering to everyone when you choose to be polarizing. Decide whom you're not going to be, and stick with it.

Exclusivity breeds a sense of collective identity. If you're one of those the brand appeals to, you're part of an exclusive club. Look at the social nature of MINI drivers, from waving at each other as they pass each other on the road to the creation of their community. For Prizeotel, it means that customers stay on the e-mail list and see updates and videos of what's going on at the hotel—a community of transient travelers. For 42Below, it means fans sending other fans the viral videos that built this brand—from insider to insider, hand to hand. For Indium, it means that technical experts talk directly to technical experts in language that only they understand.

Eliminate what's no longer necessary. Polarizing is an exercise in subtraction. Sometimes, that means you need to get out of your own way and let the people who need help talk to the people who can help them. Indium Corporation teaches us that the shortest distance between two points is the one without you in the middle.

Distillation is not just different-ness. Being different for the sake of being different is just another way of saying you lack discipline. Distillation of your brand is an exercise in making choices: what is in and what is out. What is in must still be meaningful to your audience as well as ownable by and credible for your brand. Strong brands are never caricatures. They are not exaggerations of reality. They are distillations of meaning and association.

Edgy is a tattoo. You can't remove it when your parents finally find out you got it and start yelling at you. There's nothing more contemptible than a person—or a brand—that takes a bold stand and then beats a hasty retreat at the first sign of trouble. Some will be offended. And others will tattoo your brand name on their bodies forever.

CHAPTER EIGHT: *Seize the Microphone*

Who is the personality in your market? Who speaks the loudest and has the most to say? Who is unavoidable?

You. You take up all the oxygen in the room.

It doesn't matter if you have one or more giants in your market. They may be big, but that doesn't mean they're leading the conversation. Their size doesn't make them nearer or dearer to the hearts of your core customers. Revenue doesn't equal personality, nor is market share equivalent to emotional connection. You don't have to accept that you're not big enough to be the industry spokesman, so naively grab the microphone and speak up for the whole industry. The giant hates this, but your customers love it.

You understand that it's not enough to be polite and participate. So go ahead and step up. Seize the microphone. Your audience is waiting.

One of the things that made (Product) RED a powerful idea is that they felt they were part of something bigger than just their brand. This helped a bit with the risk factor because a lot of large brands are very risk averse. We knew that we wouldn't get on Oprah *and we wouldn't be on the front page of the* Financial Times *at launch if we weren't doing something bold with some big and well-known players.*

—TAMSIN SMITH, FORMER PRESIDENT OF (PRODUCT) RED

Breaking through the clutter is often a matter of seizing the imagination of your audience. There's no shortage of demands on our attention. We're bombarded with messages, both wanted and unwanted, at all hours of the day and night. As a result, we've built higher psychological walls. We're increasingly numbed to stimulation, which in turn has spurred many unimaginative businesspeople to simply turn up their volume even louder. This is an unfortunate cycle, a death spiral of trust and engagement. How we rise above the noise is often a question of the power of our ideas rather than the size our spending.

"I'm always driven by ideas," (Product) RED's former president Tamsin Smith told me. Since its inception in 2006, (Product) RED has raised more than $150 million to date for the Global Fund, which in turn provides funding to fighting AIDS in Africa. Interestingly, its business model is licensing, not philanthropy, with up to half the profits from participating products bearing the (RED) design going to its nonprofit partner. (Product) RED's iconic presence among a carefully selected group of high-profile brands, from American Express and Apple's iPod to Converse and the Gap, as well as its high-profile founders Bobby Shriver and U2 front man Bono, has created a groundswell of awareness and cache around the idea of saving lives a world away.

"(RED)'s impact was that there was an idea that gave brands a point of view and an energy and excitement above and beyond what they'd normally encounter in their scope of business. For the Gap, it was a chance to finally connect the work that they were doing in social responsibility, compliance, and capacity-building work in sub-Saharan Africa and connect that to the consumer, in a way that was authentic and that they couldn't have done on their own. For the designers, it was their chance to feel so much more empowered and inspired by the idea behind what they were designing for once. The collections were the best things I've seen out of the Gap in a long time. It lit a fire because people want to believe in something."

How you can rise up and seize the imaginations of powerful brands—or millions of people, for that matter—comes down to the power of ideas and the passion that you can convey to them by your words and actions. Passion is contagious.

"Sometimes you can create passionate believers by being a passionate believer," Smith told me. "There are parallels in the political world in history of the little guy winning. I don't think it was simply that right was on their side but that there was something galvanizing and supremely powerful about the idea behind what they were doing that allowed them to be success-ful. Look at someone like Gandhi. He didn't go to the giants. He didn't go to the elite in India and ask, 'How are we going to get rid of the British?' He went to the people that everybody else was forgetting about, the tens of millions of downtrodden untouch-ables in the countryside, and he made them his army. In a sense, when a brand tackles what they're doing, they need the power of their army."

(Product) RED activated the giants of the world—the mega-brands and the consumers in affluent countries who buy them—on behalf of those who are so powerless they can't speak for them-selves. "There's strength to being a literal giant and having the kind of reach that those brands do. Bono used to say it was a bit of jujitsu—we were turning the biggest guys toward helping the lit-tlest guys, people who couldn't afford the forty-three cents a day to buy the pills to keep them alive. It's payback for everyone. The goal was to pay back to the brand, for our shareholders—the people in Africa—and for consumers, who would feel much greater meaning in the impact they could have from the simple act of shopping."

YOU NEED TO SEIZE imaginations before you can credibly seize the microphone, otherwise you're just more of the noise. Ideas—the right ideas, the ones that set your audience on fire with the same passion you exhibit—are more powerful than dollars. And make no mistake, the right ideas attract the dollars.

When you choose to **Seize the Microphone,** you put forward an idea so powerful that you become the conversation, the spark that captures the imagination. Think of what Smith said regarding (Product) RED and the Gap, one of the organization's keystone partners. (RED) gave brands and the consumers who buy them a point of view. It focused their attention on an issue and connected it in a meaningful and credible way to who they were. The partner brands and the consumers we see today walking down the street wearing outward trappings of their association with (RED) have self-identified as belonging to this movement.

The idea is the spark and the animation of that spark is the unavoidable presence of the brand wherever that particular customer goes. Brands that choose to **Seize the Microphone** are unavoidable because they have a sticky message that resonates with their core audience.

Often we see companies win with this strategy when their competitors are focused on each other—when most of the marketing efforts are focused on the vertical trade press and the channel. This doesn't commit you to a bank-breaking ad budget, though. When you choose to **Seize the Microphone** you commit to understanding your customer better than anyone else. You get them and they get you.

Think of this strategy as creating a discussion where none existed before—of providing that spark that didn't exist before you gave it life. You will make yourself the spokesperson for the industry, so that anyone making a buying decision in your space has to actively pick you—or actively decide not to pick you.

Regardless of their decision, you're never going to be ignored.

Being the Only Name in Town:
Go Daddy

Today, we're not only the biggest player in this industry but the fastest growing. It's a real unusual situation. The reason is that we continue to focus on making sure everybody knows we're an option—it could be for the right reason or what people think is the wrong reason—but eventually they all become our customer.

— BOB PARSONS, CEO AND FOUNDER, GO DADDY

Ask Go Daddy CEO Bob Parsons about the reactions he gets every year to his advertising and you'll hear something few advertisers will own up to. "I would rather they hate my ad than love it," Parsons told me. "It's when they're upset with an ad, and they graphically describe or exaggerate why . . . it draws so much attention to it. All these guys, these ad critics, they need to exaggerate. I have one of them who has become a dear friend of mine. Barbara Lippert is with *Adweek*. Initially, I think it was our second year, she referred to us as 'the lowest of the low.' I called Barbara and told her it was actually quite an honor. This year, she said Go Daddy was back to being lowest of the low. I called her and told her I couldn't thank her enough. And I couldn't wait to tell my mother."

Bob Parsons understands something that many marketers fail to grasp: "In some respects, it seems like I'm one of the few guys in the world who understands that ads are meant to sell stuff."

Go Daddy's decision to shift from quiet domain name registrar to cultural icon was borne of frustration. "We got to the point where we knew we had the best pricing, the widest product line, and the best products, and we knew that we had services that our competitors didn't even offer," Parsons told me. "So why in the world did we only have a 16 percent market share?" A consultancy came on board to interview current and prospective customers to understand why the company was where it was. "They came back a month or so later and said, 'The reason everyone isn't your customer is because they don't know you exist. What you need to think about is moving into mainstream media.' We said, 'OK, let's do it, and by the way, the Super Bowl is coming up.' "

The resulting strategy was unleashed on Super Bowl XXXIX viewers by way of a mock testimony commercial featuring the first Go Daddy Girl, WWE personality Candice Michelle, who stood up in the courtroom to explain how Go Daddy would be advertising its products. The stock characters acting as the approval board of the network all gasped aloud and reached for their oxygen tanks as Candice demonstrated the dance routine that clearly wasn't designed for prime-time television. But if the elderly network approvals board members on the commercial were left breathless by what they saw, so was everyone watching the Super Bowl, including every competitor in domain name registration. By the end of the evening on February 6, 2005, the Patriots had defeated the Eagles, 24 to 21. And by the morning of February 7, the first and likely only name anyone could recall in domain name registration was Go Daddy. The brand has gone on to advertise in every Super Bowl since that first spot in 2005— and each spot has used similarly provocative models in similarly contrived situations bordering on crossing every line in advertising. And yet, each year Parsons tells us in press release after press release that his Super Bowl ads are working.

"At that time, we had a market share of 16 percent—today, it's over 50 percent. Today, we're not only the biggest player in this industry but the fastest growing. It's a real unusual situation. The reason is that we continue to focus on making sure everybody knows we're an option—it could be for the right reason or what people think is the wrong reason—but eventually they all become our customer."

Go Daddy planted a flag in the market with an edgy, provocative brand image. From Parsons's opinions and commentary on his video blog to the company's NASCAR racing sponsorship and the company's rock and roll attitude, Go Daddy is unlike anything else in its space. The company's detractors call the company's commercials trashy. Their fans call them fun. Parsons calls them successful. The average consumer with a passing interest in the Internet would have been hard pressed to name any company that could provide them with a domain name prior to the 2005 Super Bowl commercial. No one had ever invested in bringing this news to the mass market. Go Daddy, with 16 percent market share, stood up and introduced itself to the biggest audience available at the time.

According to Parsons, the "decision to run the ad on the Super Bowl was as right as rain."

Let's reflect for a moment on what makes Go Daddy successful. The company prides itself on providing outstanding customer support and low prices. Go Daddy delivers an outstanding experience to its customers. But this is after the fact. What gets them in the conversation in the first place is that they are unavoidable. They are a top mention in any conversation about Web hosting. They have *become* the conversation—you either pick them because they're the only one you've ever heard of, or you actively choose not to go with them for reasons of your own.

No one seeking to register a domain name does so without making that decision. And that's the point.

If no brand is the front-runner in the minds of the average consumer, there's no reason you can't grab the microphone yourself.

What enduring lessons can we take away from Go Daddy?

- **FUN ALWAYS BEATS SMART.** You can have the most insightful reason in the world for your customer to do business with you, but if you don't capture their imagination, they'll never hear you.

- **WE LOVE CONTRASTS.** How on earth did a domain name registrar company end up with a brand image that features beautiful women, racing sponsorships, and a rock and roll attitude? Don't they understand that this brand is supposed to be for IT guys only?

- **IT'S ABOUT PEOPLE, NOT TECHNOLOGY.** People buy domain names and launch Web sites so they can run their own businesses. Parsons understood that he needed to make his company approachable, fun, and geared toward a nontechnical customer who wanted to run a business, not a Web site. So he grabbed their attention, gave them absolutely wonderful support, and showed them they could save money.

- **AUTHENTICITY, LEADERSHIP, AND MARKET STEWARDSHIP ALL MATTER.** Parsons blogs. Parsons talks on GoDaddy.com TV. He's active with congressional leaders on Capitol Hill, just as he's active in proposing measures to make domain name ownership easier. He is the spokesperson for his industry. He's honest, outspoken, and available.

Go Daddy and Bob Parsons are unavoidable. They've taken up all the oxygen in the room. This is a powerful strategy for killing giants in industries where no one has stepped up to own the hearts and minds of the end user.

Being Everywhere Young Families Are: Miki House

We simply think about what's in children's best interests and then do whatever is necessary. This is why other companies can't imitate us. We take great pride in this fact and the pride is the base of all our activities.

—KOICHI KIMURA, CEO AND FOUNDER, MIKI HOUSE

Parent-inventors are a special breed. We understand product shortcomings in a way that few product managers ever will, because when things don't work the way they're supposed to, our kids scream in our faces. "This jumper gets stuck on my great big pumpkin-size head. This is Dad's fault." That's the only enduring message you get when you're a parent and something isn't just right. If you've never been to the trade shows that cater to these markets—the ABC Show in Las Vegas, or the Kind + Jungend International Exposition in Cologne, Germany—you won't fully appreciate the length and breadth of innovation in this business.

This is what makes Miki House, the Japanese clothing manufacturer and retailer for young children, unique. Miki House's vision doesn't stop at making quality, stylish clothing for children. The company's vision is "to fill the lives of children and their families with smiles," which is grounded in their mission to "sell products that place the needs of children first, helping make a bright future for children and their families, all over the world."

Let's talk for a moment about what we don't see in these two statements: They don't say "apparel" or "retailing" or even stop at "children." They say "children and their families," "make a bright future," and "smiles."

"I want to create products which contribute to society and provide services that delight people," CEO and Founder Koichi Kimura told me. "Even though the size of the company is small, we want to be a company that people feel is irreplaceable and cannot live without."

How does this vision translate into action for Miki House? From their core business in apparel, they vertically integrated into retailing to extend their brand experience. Understanding that new parents need advice, they launched a publishing arm, producing parenting and children's books, plus a host of other titles. These efforts were precursors to on-site educational classes for children in subjects ranging from learning conversational English to playing the violin, as well as child-rearing classes for new parents. And, to make sure that "Miki House kids" had proper role models to look up to, their entry into sports sponsorships, including Athens 2004 Judo gold medalist Tadahiro Nomura, put the Miki House brand in front of millions of viewers. Miki House also owns a judo dojo, sponsors a junior yacht-racing regatta, and took a stake in alternative charter schools.

"Miki House's main mission is to create children's culture," Kimura explained. "We want to be a company not only famous for children's clothing but also relied on for whatever is needed for children."

The ecosystem is now complete: What began as a vertically integrated apparel and retailing brand expanded to encompass the immediate needs and future aspirations of parents and the dreams they have for their children. Miki House follows you from birth to your toddler years to your development as a small sentient being, providing you with a sense of style, an appreciation of quality, and the means to explore your world and prepare for your future.

What enduring lessons can we take away from Miki House?

- **BECOME UNAVOIDABLE BY APPEARING EVERYWHERE YOUR TARGET MARKET LOOKS FOR HELP.** Ensure that everything you do lives within the same value-driven philosophy underlying your core brand. "We want to become an indispensable presence in the lives of the families we serve," Kimura explained. "We want to give something back to society by supporting children's dreams in a whole variety of ways."

- **EACH VENTURE SUPPORTS THE OTHER.** See how apparel supports retailing, how sports sponsorships support publishing, how school ownership supports in-store classes, and so forth.

- **DREAMS ARE MORE POWERFUL THAN ENTERTAINMENT.** Is there anything silly about Miki House? No. The Miki House brand image springs from the sense of personal accomplishment. There is a sense of camaraderie in overcoming challenges, from practicing judo to studying a foreign language, that runs like a thread through Miki House's branding values and separates it from your garden variety "kids company."

Kimura sums it up like this: "There are many competitors in the world that produce apparel, but a company like Miki House, which can provide real culture, including education, books, and other children-related goods and services, is not so common. I am always conscious of exporting not only goods but also Miki House culture to the world."

Creating Passionate Believers by Being
Passionate Believers:
Fiskars

We didn't want to do a "buzz" campaign. We wanted to cre-
ate a movement. We wanted to change people, to partner with
them and become part of that conversation. We definitely took
the hard road.

—SUZANNE FANNING, DIRECTOR OF COMMUNICATIONS, FISKARS

How does the second oldest incorporated company in the world
reverse its declining fortunes in an increasingly commoditized
business? One Fiskateer at a time.

Fiskars has been making edged tools—axes, saws, scissors, and other cutting implements—in their hometown of Fiskars, Finland, for more than 360 years. Their iconic orange color
makes them unmistakable alongside their unbranded competitors from the aisles of mass merchants to specialty retailers
across the world to the Museum of Modern Art. But when big
box retailers began to cut back on shelf space in favor of lower-
cost competitors, Fiskars took a long look at its brand equity and
knew it had a problem.

"Our research told us that people rarely mentioned Fiskars
by name," Suzanne Fanning, director of communications at Fiskars, explained to me. "It was rarely emotional or passionate."
Looking specifically at the scrapbooking and crafting market
that relied on their scissors and other cutting products, the company knew there was a lot of passion and emotion surrounding
this hobby, but Fiskars wasn't part of the dialogue. "We weren't
a player in this discussion. We were viewed as just a tool."

The company launched a multifaceted campaign to reengage
with these scrapbookers and crafters, including a redesign of

their Web site with expert demonstrations, user-generated videos, how-tos, chat, and a host of other activities to close the loop with end users. "To take things a step further, we decided to launch a brand ambassador campaign." At this stage, Fanning decided what she didn't want to do: "We didn't want to do a 'buzz' campaign. We wanted to create something genuine. We wanted to create a movement. We wanted to change people, to partner with them and become part of that conversation. We definitely took the hard road."

Her introduction to agency Brains on Fire sparked the idea of the Fiskateers. Spike Jones, then Brains on Fire's head "Firestarter," explained how Fiskars approached his company. "The Fiskars team said, 'We make scissors, we make paper cutters, we make tools—there's no emotional connection there.' " Jones continued: "They asked consumers, 'If Fiskars were a beverage, what would we be?' People said milk. 'If Fiskars were a snack food, what would we be?' Crackers! The good news is that we all can open up our refrigerators and find these things, but there's a problem. They make these great tools, people think that they're great, but no one's talking about them because there's no emotional connection there."

The brand ambassador program was launched, and the first of the company's Fiskateers were carefully selected. "We wanted to have a genuine crafter-to-crafter connection," Fanning explained. "We didn't want to hire some fancy professional who would look down on them or thought they were up on a pedestal. We wanted someone who was right there with them so they would feel like Fiskars was their friend. We didn't want a spokesperson." In the words of Spike Jones, "Influence can be created, but passion cannot."

Fiskateers are recruited one by one through personal contact with lead Fiskateers on their Web site. Membership isn't automatic. Each must explain in detail why they want to join the movement. Once they're in, they go through a thorough indoctrination process including training in not only product expertise but in what it means to be a brand ambassador. Each commits to a Fiskateer Oath. And each gets the ultimate trapping of authority, a unique pair of Fiskars scissors, replete with a custom handle and an engraved membership number on the blade. A Fiskateer's scissor is a badge, not a casual trade show give-away.

Once a Fiskateer comes on board, they run workshops on scrapbooking, interact with hobbyists in the community, and act as official Fiskars demonstrators. What they don't do is push product. "Fiskateers never walk in with a sell sheet . . . they never blog about anything they don't want to," Fanning told me. Their role is crystal clear. Being an ambassador means spreading goodwill.

Is the program a success? After a Fiskateer visit to a store, sales increases are double that of comparable stores. The program, which began in 2002 with four Fiskateers and a goal of 250, now boasts more than six thousand. The company targeted a 10 percent increase in online brand chatter—it achieved 600 percent. Where the company hoped to have four geographic locations covered, it now has Fiskateers in all fifty states plus in seventy other countries around the world.

But the results go further than that. "They spend less money on R&D," Jones explained, "because engineering turns to the community and says, 'What are the new colors this year?' and the community tells them. 'Can you name this product?' and the community names the product." Fiskars has done more than just run demos across the country. They've become the face of scrapbooking and crafting for thousands of fans across the country.

What enduring lessons can we take away from Fiskars?

- **"INFLUENCE CAN BE CREATED. PASSION CANNOT."** Creating a campaign that relies on face-to-face personal interactions means you are relying on infectious enthusiasm. We know when people are interested. It's hard to fake.

- **SOCIAL DOESN'T HAVE TO MEAN TECHNOLOGY.** Creating a sticky, vibrant, long-living ambassador program is an exercise in execution. The Fiskars program gives us a number of important clues: passion over expertise and influence, face-to-face over automation, and mindshare over rapid dissemination. Creating a social movement requires good manners. Fiskars couldn't have done this with a Facebook page.

- **AMBASSADORS VERSUS EXPERTS VERSUS DEMONSTRATORS.** In areas of subjectivity—of taste—passion will always win over expertise. In areas of objectivity—of fact—passion without expertise is disastrous. I will consider advice from a passionate brand ambassador on the subject of music, food, or fashion. If I need my computer fixed or want to consider different medical procedures or legal options—I need expertise. Knowing what you're selling and how your market perceives you is a mandatory first step here.

Fiskars and their happy band of Fiskateers show us that passion begets more passion. By bringing people who weren't "celebrities"—regular people like the brand's core audience—and who were deeply passionate about the art of crafting, Fiskars reignited their brand's relevance to the resurging crafts movement, and created an entire ecosystem of evangelists, both inside the company and out.

Key Takeaways

We've discussed companies from different continents with different cultures and industry dynamics. Yet all show us how you can be the player the other guys just can't ignore.

The ideas are bigger than the categories. What's the difference between selling domain names to IT professionals and showing everyone at home that it's fun to have your own business? One is an arm's-length transaction, while the other is an exhortation, an offer to show you the way it's done. When our vision is bigger, our voice is bigger.

Bob Parsons and Go Daddy show us that you, too, can have the personal freedom to say what you have to say, launch your own blog or e-business, and just have fun—all without being an IT guy. His ads, regardless of whether you love them or hate them, show us the freedom and fun that your own business can give you. He isn't selling domain names—he's selling freedom.

Miki House's Koichi Kimura tells us that young minds need to be surrounded by meaning—from the quality of their clothing to the quality of their experiences. It's about supporting the youngest members of society with things that will help them grow and come to appreciate the right things in life, from accomplishment to hard work and dedication. He isn't selling clothes—he's selling dreams.

What about Fiskars? Is this really a hardware story? Suzanne Fanning and her Fiskateers show us that hobbies are personal, not sterile products or even personalities. Fiskars isn't selling crafting supplies—they're selling passion.

In the absence of a spokesperson, be the spokesperson. In the absence of personality, show some personality. Even if it's not expected. Especially if it's not expected.

Go Daddy was a 16 percent market share player when they ran their first Super Bowl ad, announcing to an audience of millions who weren't quite sure what a domain name was that you could buy one and launch your own Web site very affordably. Have you ever heard another domain name company's voice before?

Miki House thought it natural to offer an educational curriculum, open charter schools, and sponsor athletes. They didn't turn to partners to do this, but knew that unless they did this themselves, these efforts would fall on deaf ears.

Fiskars was competing with no-brand OEM products designed

for cost, not quality. They knew that crafting was personal and important to its fans. So they stepped up and tapped these same fans to become the face of the company to millions of others.

If your industry is dominated by giants who are focused on each other, go talk to your customers. This doesn't always take big budgets, as we've seen here. Understand them better than your giants do, interact with them, and speak their language better than anyone else can.

Domain name registrars didn't talk to consumers. They only talked to IT people in clean, B2B settings. The leaders in this business fought among themselves, jockeying for position. Go Daddy spoke to everyone, loudly.

Miki House didn't just make clothing. They expanded to be everywhere their customers needed help. In the process, they forged a culture driven by feedback and customer insight.

Fiskateers not only interact daily with the crafting market, they are the crafting market. This movement has become the eyes and ears of the company, providing the insights that traditional marketing research would have to pay top dollar to glimpse.

You can make yourself indispensable by making yourself impossible to miss. Does a customer looking to buy a domain name ignore Go Daddy? No—they may actively choose not to buy from Go Daddy for their own reasons, but Go Daddy is impossible to ignore. They are the first name to come up and that makes them part of every buying decision.

Miki House is there with you as your young family grows. It has roots throughout the lives of Japanese children.

Fiskars is physically present, mingling with the crafting community on a daily basis. If you're a crafter, you run into Fiskars enough to make them top of mind.

Social means personal. Creating a bond with other passionate people—your brand's representatives as well as your brand's customers and fans—takes meaningful interaction over time. There are no shortcuts, but there are lessons to be learned.

CHAPTER NINE: *All the Wood Behind the Arrow(s)*

There's always an opponent even the giant doesn't want to fight. The southpaw who can throw an uppercut, the scrapper who messes up their timing, or maybe the accessories brand that owns four feet of linear space in too many of their national retailers. When natural ability and dedication have forged a pair of specialized weapons, you become an opponent the giant is reluctant to face.

All the wood behind the arrows? Is there more than one arrow? Yes, always. One arrow is never enough. Develop primary strengths in a pair of important areas and you become the competitor the giant is more than happy to avoid.

Epaminondas said, "This is our tradition. This is the one thing we have to do. If we can make the Spartans turn around relatively quickly and run away, nothing else matters. It doesn't matter if we are eventually out-flanked. This is what matters." And he was right.

—DR. J. E. LENDON, PROFESSOR OF CLASSICAL STUDIES, UNIVERSITY OF VIRGINIA, AND AUTHOR OF *SOLDIERS AND GHOSTS*

Epaminondas, the king of Thebes and commander of all Boeotian forces, knew that a stand-up fight against the legendary Spartan infantry was a losing proposition.

In the spring of 371 BC, he prepared for battle against the advice of his generals, who strongly advised him to withdraw. The polis of Thebes had been embroiled in an endless war with their ancient enemies for generations, and now he faced the Spartan warrior elite on the plains of Leuctra. But Epaminondas, the best man of his age, had different plans for the Spartans. He would attack them where they were strongest—"crush the head of the serpent"—and send the rest of their allies to flight.

A moment's reflection will help us better understand this moment in history. The Greeks waged war throughout antiquity with Homer's *Iliad* as their playbook. The ideals of personal valor and honor—of fearlessness and discipline—held the Greek fighter in check. Wars were fought according to strict customs: Two blocks of opposing soldiers faced each other in tightly packed *phalanxes*. Discussions were held to determine whether the armies would fight this day or not. When conditions were favorable, the two came together—a rugby scrum with spears. These battles lasted for hours, with long intermittent pauses for everyone to catch their breath. At some point, one side gave way and ran. The winner was the one who held the field.

Further, for most of the Greek city-states, armies were comprised of citizen soldiers who tended farms and orchards all year and only did their civic duty to train for war occasionally. Only the Spartans fielded a professional army, preferring to leave the manual labor of agriculture to its helot class of slaves. This dedication to arms was readily apparent on the battlefield. It was common knowledge that the longer the fight wore on, the more skill, discipline, and endurance would tilt the odds in Sparta's favor.

Epaminondas couldn't match the professional army of Sparta man for man. The polis of Thebes couldn't afford the sheer cost of a full-time professional soldier class. But it could afford to create a select group of professional soldiers—a Sacred Band of three hundred—that could form the tip of the spear. He couldn't afford a headlong fight in the traditional form, with each army forming up its elite on the honored right flank to crush the relatively weaker left of its opponent, only to pinwheel around to finally grind out the endgame. But he could borrow a page from his predecessor, Pagondas, who once stacked the Theban phalanx twenty-five men deep, as opposed to the traditional eight, and stack his men fifty deep to ensure he could punch through the Spartan line. And he could form up his army with his elite Sacred Band on the left flank, turning the traditional reward system of Greek warfare on its head, to face the superior Spartan right wing.

"All of these things together allowed him to 'crush the head of the serpent,' as he said himself, and drive the Spartans away," Dr. J. E. Lendon, professor of classical studies at University of Virginia, told me. "Once the Spartans were on the run—once you saw the good people running, morale being as important as it was in such situations—everybody else ran away as quickly as they could. So away they went."

Epaminondas melded his own cultural forces with a counterintuitive flipped strategy, a real strategic master stroke, to win the day. "Each of these ideas was interesting. The fifty-deep phalanx is an example of learning from his predecessor, Pagondas. This was a 'putting all the eggs in one basket' strategy. If we do this, unless we win in the first ten minutes, we're not going to have a first fifteen minutes. And these battles would go on for many hours, so the normal assumption was that you'd have to set up for the long haul. Stacking his phalanx on the left was an interesting thing because that was new. Epaminondas was the first. This is like the CEO switching offices with the mail-room guy."

Dr. Lendon explained that Epaminondas had to make a clear

distinction between the expected rewards system of his day and what he needed of his army this day. "He said, we are the best guys but we're going to do something more important. We're going to do it another way." After all, once the CEO decides to sit in a cubicle, honor goes to everyone else who also chooses to sit in a cubicle.

Epaminondas sets the stage for us and shows that you can defeat a giant—even one as feared as Sparta—if you can overwhelm them in a small number of critical areas. For the Boeotians, this meant stacking the phalanx fifty-men deep and placing them on a left flank led by a select group of experts in order to overwhelm the enemy where they were strongest.

Crush the head of the serpent. And send the rest into panic.

EPAMINONDAS LIVED WITHIN A cultural legacy of the Theban "deep phalanx." His tactical choice of arraying this formation on the nontraditional left flank was his stroke of genius. The Sacred Band gave him the strength at that point of contact to put his plan in motion.

None of these steps alone would have unseated the Spartans and their allies at Leuctra. The giant didn't get to be this big by getting pushed around by anybody. It takes a rare combination of abilities executed with skill to win and hold contested ground. It's always more than just one thing.

So what characterizes the right combination of skills?

Successful companies often start with one skill deeply entrenched in their culture—in heritage, or passion, or the deep values that they hold close. This first idea often came from other industries or previous lives that may at first seem a bit out of place in its current setting. A brand that brings a personal care mind-set to the household cleaner industry, like Method does, exemplifies this ideal.

Second, we see a functional strength that's meaningful to

one of the brand's key stakeholders, either the channel or the end user, which delivers this core belief in a vivid way. Again with Method, we clearly see the company's mission to provide cleaning products that are good for the planet—that are sustainable, green formulations—and consumers respond to this. Together, there is *brand tension*—a dynamic that is complex but complementary, that stands the test of both time and external pressure. Complex brands hold mystery and are therefore difficult to unseat.

It's never one thing. There is always something else, a tempering second element, which makes the whole come together.

A Passion for Sustainability and a Focus on User Experience: Method

There was no way I could be successful in the long run if I launched a single-attribute brand. The giants would have figured us out.

—ERIC RYAN, COFOUNDER OF METHOD

When two people from radically different perspectives decide to create something, the results are unpredictable. Perhaps this is why so many successful brands come from a pair of founders. This disruptive element is often what's needed in a slow-moving, deeply entrenched industry like household cleaners. Just look at Method, a brand that has grown to more than $100 million in revenue built on the twin prongs of sustainability and product design, both converging to deliver a user experience unlike any other in the world of cleaning products.

"I was surprised to learn how dirty cleaning products were,"

Method cofounder Eric Ryan told me. "The guiding light was about how the world should be—how the cleaning world should be." Where most companies are started out of the personal frustrations of a founder, Eric and cofounder Adam Lowry saw the opportunity to do something right for the planet and right for consumers. Making, as Ryan called it, "a simple act of appropriation," Method became "Aveda for the home." "The big idea was connecting lifestyle to the home. No one likes to clean. It's mundane. So it's our job to make it a little more enjoyable."

Method's slogan is "People Against Dirty." The company makes environmentally conscious cleaning products for the home that not only smell good but also come in extraordinarily well-designed containers. Your soap looks good on your countertop. Your detergent doesn't smell like chemicals. And they leave no toxic residue on your dishes, fixtures—or children.

The design of the containers themselves is the first thing a user is likely to notice. Designer Karim Rashid was brought in at the company's launch in 2001 to consult on the brand and design the first suite of products. "They were a couple of unknown guys with a little company in a mundane industry dominated by much bigger players," Rashid told me. "I saw so much potential immediately. I have always believed that young entrepreneurs are savvier to our changing world and to new markets." As for the products themselves, Rashid noted, "The objects are sensual, easy to use, innovative . . . they use recyclable materials, they're designed to fit into contemporary spaces, and the contents are all organic and biodegradable—this is how all products should be. Each is designed for its specific use and context, but the overall branding is retained through minimal sensual aesthetics, colors, and graphic treatments."

Once past the design aesthetics of the container, however, the user quickly notices a difference. Method products don't feel like other products. Ryan's simple act of appropriation brought a personal care product sensibility to a category dominated by heavy bottles full of harsh-smelling liquids. "We are a brand that delivers a better experience," he told me. "That's delivered in multiple ways from personality to fragrance to formula."

Method's "greenness" is an important element of the overall picture, but it is never viewed as the company's sole mission. "Green is part of what we do and we do it because it's the right thing to do and we can take advantage of that from time to time in our marketing where appropriate—but it's ultimately not how we compete as a business," Ryan relates. It's the brand tension—this internal complexity that balances physical design with formulation to create the unmistakable Method user experience—that gives Method its uniqueness.

Method's 2010 launch of laundry detergent captures both elements neatly: a super-concentrated plant-based formulation in a pump bottle designed for one finger use, dramatically smaller than the equivalent sized competitive product, with enough detergent to clean fifty loads of laundry. The end user experience is delivered through the packaging and human factors convenience, while the sustainable philosophy comes through via the attention to reducing packaging materials as well as the plant-based formulation.

Could Method have happened if it were an internal initiative launched at a major consumer packaged goods giant? "No, definitely not," Ryan answered me. "If it did, they would look at the business as an insider. They would know too much. They would have accepted the way it was defined and moved on. I was naive to cleaning. I was able to not recognize that this is how the game is played. I looked outside the category and said you could treat cleaning the way you treated personal care." In summing up the unique brand tension that stretches from a design aesthetic to user experience to sustainability, Ryan told me, "There was no way I could be successful in the long run if I launched a single-attribute brand. The giants would have figured us out."

What enduring lessons can we take away from Method?

- **METHOD IS A COMPANY WRAPPED AROUND A PHILOSOPHY.** Does this seem counterintuitive? It shouldn't be. While many brands are supply chains with a veneer of "branding," Method's practices are self-defining. From the company's Web site to its packaging designs to its hiring practices, office space, and communications, everything this brand does is consistent with its core philosophy.

- **BRAND TENSION CREATES INTEREST, COMPLEXITY, AND ILLUSIVENESS.** Method's attributes of sustainability and user experience are complementary—people who gravitate to design don't find sustainability and environmental responsibility offensive. Each supports and reinforces the other. But look at it from the giant's perspective: complex, interesting brands are much harder to carbon copy and knock-off. This makes them much trickier to fight.

- **SHIFT THE CONVERSATION.** Looking at the daunting competitive landscape the company faces, Ryan teaches us to focus the message in a place where the giant can't. "What are the legacy issues? What are the things we'll never win on? We push them aside. Then, we look for the things that we can talk about or make matter. Our competition will either not talk about it because they can't get there or they won't waste their breath talking about it because they can't justify taking the time on it."

Method is a study in building a friendly, engaging, and complex brand that has carved out a sustainable niche for itself in an industry space dominated by giants. If it had focused on design alone, it wouldn't have worked. The market is similarly littered with "green" products, both from upstarts as well as from the giants themselves. The combination of factors is what makes Method such an important story.

The Evolutionary Shift from Space Management to Category Stewardship: Belkin

All of a sudden, there was complexity of connectivity, complexity of managing shelf space, of managing profitability, of supply chain issues . . . because retailers were growing so fast, they needed their partners to help them navigate some of these issues for them because they couldn't do it themselves.

—MARK REYNOSO, CEO OF BELKIN

Once upon a time, Belkin was easy to ignore. They didn't really compete in the technology categories that you cared about, sticking to adaptors and curly cords of various lengths. When they began their emergence from the lower depths of the consumer electronics accessories space, they did so with simple add-ons, a corded headset here and a USB hub there. By the time you realized that this bits-and-pieces vendor had grown from four feet of dedicated linear space on the retail shelf to eight, it was really too late. Belkin was an insidious competitor to face, which makes them a great story.

"If you go back to the late nineties, you had traditional retail going through puberty and entering adulthood," Belkin CEO Mark Reynoso told me. "These retailers—Best Buy, Circuit City, CompUSA—were adding stores at a fast clip, bigger stores at a fast clip, and the industry was beginning to expand the market by adding on accessories and peripherals. Consumer electronics was no longer just a computer and a printer." The traditional consumer electronics giants—and only one of the above three is alive and well today—were flexing their new muscles in concert with a dramatically expanding assortment of devices and solutions. But with that explosion of newness came change—not just in the products but in the ways that retailers and consumers had to process it all.

Belkin today provides peripherals and accessories for a wide variety of products—from iPhones and iPads to laptops and home theater systems. The incredible variety of Belkin products is itself a testament to the evolution of this fast-changing environment. The company's earliest days were spent managing a complex tangle of cables and other subassemblies that no retailer really wanted to fully comprehend. They were more than happy to have Belkin simply manage the entire section for them, making the product assortment and merchandising decisions on their behalf—and Belkin was happy to oblige them. This practice of space management was common among consumer packaged goods companies and their brokers, who had resources dedicated to planning out the retail shelf blueprints—the planograms—that determined which products sat on which peg hooks on which aisles in each store across the country. But for a consumer electronics brand working within this fairly unsophisticated channel, this was rare. This gave Belkin a unique amount of leeway within this competitive space, and consequently made them hard to displace. Building a center of expertise in space management would prove to be a very important strategic decision on Belkin's part.

As the consumer electronics industry began to mature and their rapid store openings and expansions began to cool, the emphasis began to shift from the management of the products already on the store's shelves to what was coming next. "Our strength in space management that was so critical during this growth spurt was less critical once the industry began to mature," Reynoso related to me. "Retailers were less focused on growth and more on optimization. Their mandate was to grow profitability through their existing footprint. Now, our category management moved from profit per square foot to teaching them where their categories were going." The ecosystem began to evolve from space management, the practice dedicated to managing how retail assortments were best assembled, to full category management, where a brand plays a more consultative role as futurist and forecaster. An example of Belkin's newer focus on category management is its creation in 2004 of a suite of accessories for laptops purchased for home use. "There's a laptop in the house that never leaves the house," Reynoso told me. "Compare that to the mobile warrior's laptop. You've got the New York to LA laptop and the upstairs downstairs laptop. It goes from the family room to the bedroom to the living room. But look at the accessory ecosystem around them, and they were all geared toward the mobile warriors. All black bags and ten keypads. We identified a new space, created a category of solutions around them, educated our retailers on the opportunity— we worked with Dell to fully understand this space—we took a zero revenue business and are now number one or number two in the business. And this is north of a $200 million business."

Belkin shows us an example of a brand that began with a needed and admittedly unsexy functional skill of space management, helping its retailers manage its shelves correctly, and evolved from these modest beginnings to also become the trusted guide that retailers rely on to understand the blizzard of technological change coming their way.

What enduring lessons can we take away from Belkin?

- **DO THE FUNCTIONAL DIRTY WORK THAT OTHERS BELIEVE IS BENEATH THEM**. Become a necessary part of your channel's operational system. If you can become impossible to kill, your chances for long-term survival improve.

- **GROW FROM THIS IMPORTANT PIVOT POINT OUTWARD**. From space management to category management, from managing complexity of accessories to complexity of technological change. Belkin is still providing management services to the channel— they're just doing it in a larger capacity than they used to. Can you think of a better way to boost credibility over time than being a long-term trusted adviser?

- **SEIZE THE CHOKE POINTS IN THE CHANNEL, MAKE YOURSELF INDIS-PENSIBLE TO THEM, AND CONSUMER PULL WILL FOLLOW.** Distribution is oxygen. You can't win if you're not in the room. So ensuring that you stay in the room, while others come and go, is a valuable survival strategy.

Belkin shows us how to take a pragmatic, tactical skill set, an area of functional expertise, and grow it into a trusted strategic role. Category management didn't take the place of space management—the company still performs these services today, where requested—rather, category management simply grew up around it and took it to a higher level of visibility and importance to its shrinking pool of key retailers. This is a case study in putting all the wood behind the twin arrows of functional expertise and tightly defined strategic vision, all aimed at the strategic choke point of the channel.

Disruptively Authentic: Schweitzer Engineering

The reason I like to be an engineer is that I like to take science, math, and technology and put it all together and create some value for a customer and solve a problem. It didn't seem ethical or right to charge to the market just to make a lot of money.

—DR. EDMUND SCHWEITZER, FOUNDER AND CEO OF SCHWEITZER ENGINEERING LABORATORIES

How disruptive was Dr. Edmund Schweitzer's first digital protective relay? It was one-eighth the size and one-tenth the weight of the old way of doing things, plus it could tell you that you had a malfunction on a power line exactly 45.5 miles from your substation, which on a hundred-mile stretch of line means you know exactly where your problem is, saving you a considerable amount of time, trouble, and expense to fix. In addition, his solution sold for one-third the price of those other systems his solution was on the way to replacing.

"Why not price it at $20,000 like the rest of the market instead of $6,500?" Schweitzer rhetorically asked. "My answer was, 'Because I can.' "

Schweitzer Engineering Laboratories manufactures the protective relays that prevent blackouts and other problems in the power systems that deliver electricity to cities across the world. The company's story begins with the inventor whose name it bears. Edmund Schweitzer studied electromechanical relays in college and found them fascinating. "I realized that the protective relays that protect the power system are fascinating electromechanical wonders. These are beautiful, beautiful things." His first job out of school was with the Department of Defense, conducting research on digital signal processing, but his real calling was pulling him in a different direction. "I really wanted to invent and design and manufacture products that would somehow make the world a better place," he told me. "So I was very motivated in this spirit of engineering to make things better and more economical than ever before. And working for the government wasn't the place to do that."

The spark that became his namesake company was struck by the timely intersection of his interests and the birth of the microprocessor. "It occurred to me that protective relays were very special purpose signal processors. The microprocessor was just invented—little four-bit things used in calculators. I had my signal processing background from my government work. And I wondered if we couldn't take these microprocessors and digital signal processing and put them together to do power system protection." This became the topic of his PhD dissertation and the impetus of his entrepreneurial start.

Schweitzer's solution, a digital protective relay, was a radically different take on the existing industry solutions from industrial powerhouses Westinghouse and GE. His early sales efforts didn't always meet with success, but they proved to be an important process. "I learned a lot from these calls. If you put this relay in, you'll be able to communicate with it—in 1983 the idea that you could put something out there in a substation with a modem in it and call it up was new. The first ten to twenty systems were sold as pure fault locators. But people got interested in them because every time it located a fault, it would generate a complete record of the voltages and the current, so people could see how it operated. In a short time, a year or two, people moved from using them as fault locators to using them as actual protective relays."

As with any disruptive product, close customer contact was needed to ensure everything was working the way it was supposed to. And through these early days of trial, a sense of mutual trust grew. "We had to be sure that we stayed close with the customers—they were trying something new—and we still are close, even with our first customers. We learn from each other. I tell you what, those first relays, they worked, but they weren't perfect. Today, they're excellent, but in those days I'm not embarrassed to say there were things we didn't understand." This attitude gave the company not only its initial customer base but set the philosophical tone for the company's growth ever since.

Schweitzer Engineering Laboratories developed a disruptive product, but the world is littered with bold new solutions that would have upset the incumbent apple cart if only they hadn't failed. Schweitzer succeeded not only because of a disruptively low price and a feature set that was unlike any his competitors could match. He also instilled a degree of trust, based on mutual reliance, which earned his place in his customers' substations. This trust is readily apparent in the company's policy never to charge for repairs. "Problems are rain from heaven—if you get to that root cause, if you learn from it, you make better products."

What enduring lessons can we learn from Schweitzer Engineering?

- **IF YOU LISTEN, YOUR CUSTOMERS WILL TELL YOU WHO YOU ARE.** To SEL, the solution was a radically better protective relay. To its initial customers, it was a fault detection solution. Stranger things have happened than being successful for reasons other than those you planned on.

- **TRUST IS BUILT ON CREDIBILITY, AND CREDIBILITY COMES FROM ACTING IN OTHERS' INTERESTS BEFORE YOUR OWN.** Pricing the solution low "because you can" is a remarkable statement. Could you guess that the company is privately held and has no venture capital investors? Dr. Schweitzer's statement is something that would cause the average MBA to get the vapors but is music to the ears of any company founder spending his or her own money. Never charging your customers for repairs builds trust; it sends the signal that you see the company-customer relationship as a partnership.

Schweitzer Engineering shows us how you can resoundingly win in a few key areas—with an important twist. He was selling a radically different digital protective relay that happened to have a fault detection feature; his customers were buying a superior fault detector that happened to also be a digital protective relay. You can have the world's best and most technologically disruptive solution ready to launch—"the best with the most for the least"—and still fail. But if you listen carefully, which Dr. Schweitzer certainly did on his early morning calls from his basement office—you might pick up on the right angle. Combine this with mutual trust rooted in the company's "because I can" pricing model and you have a quiver of arrows ready to fire.

Key Takeaways

Smart brands put **All the Wood Behind the Arrow(s)** by developing core competitive advantages in a few select areas to win at the point of attack and maintain their market presence against great odds and greater giants. What key takeaways can we extract from these companies?

Culture comes from you. Where you find your cultural heritage, your deep passion for an area of excellence, is a deeply personal choice. You may be committed to doing the right thing for planet earth and you may simply find electromagnetic protective relays to be "beautiful, beautiful things."

The core of Method's business resides in their deeply felt belief that there should be a better way to clean. This wasn't an idea that sprung from a research panel but from a personal conviction on the part of its founders that the world wasn't right without a sustainable, ecologically sound detergent—and one that happened to smell nice and come in an attractive package, too.

Ed Schweitzer saw beauty in electromagnetic protective relays. His calling came to him very clearly, and after speaking with him, it seemed that it would have been impossible for him to have chosen a direction in life too far from this area. He didn't gouge his customers. He wanted the product to help people. The brand's culture was firmly rooted in honesty and integrity.

This isn't a decision made from marketing research. This comes from your sense of who you are, no matter whether you were born a Boeotian or an engineer. Your culture is your soul.

Functional expertise is something that comes from what you do for others. Whatever you choose to excel in, it has to matter to your customers or channel partners. Belkin became the go-to resource for space management and planogram development for many of its key consumer electronics retailers. Once in and expertly handling this complex and slightly magical task, it would take a gaff of biblical proportions to throw them out. They became necessary. And from this trust, they grew into a larger role of category counselor and trusted adviser.

Method became the flag bearer for the "clean detergent" category by virtue of its formulation and its attention to customer experience. Without the experience, the formulation would have been ignored as just another unknown brand—while without the formulation, the user experience would have likely missed a large part of its intended market.

The protective relays that Schweitzer Engineering developed did things that no other alternative in the world could do—their fault-detection capability was utterly unique.

Your functional expertise is your craft, your vocation.

Focus the message in a place the giant can't. Winning in one particular spot means choosing to dominate a discussion the giant doesn't want to contest. How do you shift the conversation away from points the giant is going to win? This is easier said than done, of course, but it's still a road you need to travel. What are the giant's legacy issues? What are the things you'll never win on? Our job here is to push them aside and look for the things that the giant cannot or will not discuss.

Method lives in the shadow of massively larger brands, but its "competitive insulation" comes from knowing with enough certainty that its giants can't really afford to spend too much time fighting a fight that doesn't have a giant-size payoff.

Belkin, too, resides in a place where its history as category management provider makes it hard to replace. You just don't need two people assisting you with your planogram.

Schweitzer's tight focus makes it a difficult target for one of its heavily diversified giants to casually attack. Again, it simply isn't worth the effort—and the gain, for a multibillion-dollar global giant, just isn't big enough.

No one ever loses because they were too close to the

customer. How well do you listen? Is your market telling you something different than you want to hear? Are they buying based on something you never thought was important? Ed Schweitzer tells us something very important in his story. It would have been easy for him to interrupt his prospects and redirect them back to his main selling points when they expressed too much interest in the fault detection functionality of his switches. He didn't, though—he listened and adapted to what his market was telling him, opening up an opportunity that he and his company would go on to own. Our job is to listen carefully because we're all creatures of habit—we tend to hear what we want to hear and we don't always listen when we're being told the truth.

Ed Schweitzer, as well, discusses his company's constant communication and collaboration with customers, beginning in his early days of "working things out together." This humility and authenticity isn't the norm, it's the exception in most of business.

Putting all the wood behind the arrows doesn't mean you will always use the same arrows. Every market matures, with some skill sets coming to the fore and others receding over time. Your market's needs change. What is the next logical evolution of your functional expertise?

CHAPTER TEN: *Show Your Teeth*

In the back of every giant's mind is a nagging fear. The fear is that they'll be called out in public and forced to fight against an upstart who they know, in their heart of hearts, is better than they are.

The giant has more people, more money, and more market clout, but there's a hole in their confidence that the right kind of competitor keeps making bigger.

When you know you're better—and can prove it—say it early and often. Give the giant's fear a name and a very public face.

> *The feeling I had was overwhelming. I didn't get out of his way. I knew right then, that's what you have to do. That's not part of the game of football. How I felt that day, I was so proud of myself. I didn't get out of his way.*
>
> —PAT FISCHER, SEVENTEEN-YEAR NFL VETERAN CORNERBACK FOR THE ST. LOUIS CARDINALS AND THE WASHINGTON REDSKINS

In a league of tough guys, Pat Fischer was universally known as a tough guy. When Hall of Fame quarterback Johnny Unitas was asked who the new kid playing cornerback for the Redskins was, he was reported to have said, "That *kid* is Pat Fischer . . . and if he hits you, he'll knock your socks off."

In 1961, Fischer learned, to his surprise, that he'd been drafted by the St. Louis Cardinals, getting picked in the seventeenth round of the draft. His new team was surprised too, apparently, as they were unable to find pads to fit the five foot nine cornerback for several days. Fischer would go on to play in a storied defense with teammates Jerry Wilson and Herb Adderley that featured the then-revolutionary safety blitz—the first time a safety was used to rush the quarterback on an obvious passing down. Wilson's toughness combined with Adderley's sheer speed put Fischer in an awkward situation. "Our defensive coordinator told me I had to play closer to the line—I tried, but I didn't have the kind of quickness to do this," Fischer told me. "He said, if I couldn't do it, I could catch the bus and go home. So I did the only thing I could do—I moved up to the line. When I played, as long as the receiver was in front of me, I could hit them. It disrupted every offense." And so the bump-and-run defense was born.

Pat Fischer was always the underdog. He described lining up against the premier pass receivers of his day, including the first time he went up against Cleveland's Bobby Mitchell, and how he overcame his inner fear of the superbly athletic receiver by grabbing Mitchell and throwing him to the ground on the first snap—drawing a personal foul for the play. He recalled lining up twice a year against the Philadelphia Eagles' six foot nine Harold Carmichael, and against whom I took to be the most feared member of all, Bob Hayes of the Dallas Cowboys, called "the world's fastest man" by virtue of his then–world record performance winning the gold medal in the one hundred meter sprint at the Tokyo Olympics in 1964 and an adversary Fischer considered to be always one play away from winning the game. Fischer discussed what it was like when cornerbacks were football players first and pass defenders second, having to face Cleveland's Hall of Fame running back Jim Brown, a punishing runner well over two hundred pounds, coming around the end toward him. But when I asked him who he, as a pro football legend known for toughness, considered to be a tough guy, the well-rehearsed stories abruptly stopped and we found ourselves at the heart of the matter.

"I have an older brother Cletus," Fischer began. "He was a great football player at Nebraska, played one year for the Giants. Who was my high school coach? Kenny Fischer. Where's Rex? He's the second oldest, he was All Big Eight at Nebraska. They were all great football players." The genetic underpinnings of his legendary toughness were clear, being the youngest of six boys in his family. But his own emergence as a tackler came when he was eight years old in the backyard, playing football against his big brothers and their friends, when one of those neighborhood kids took the ball on an end around and decided that young Pat was the path of least resistance.

"I was in the third or fourth grade. Somewhere in there, in that backyard, against these bigger kids . . . I refused to get out of his way. He just ran over me. Such a collision. We both ended up in the bushes. I had bruises on my face. And I got up and I was the proudest little kid ever. The feeling I had was overwhelming. I didn't get out of his way. But I thought about it—he was running so hard—his leg scratched up my face . . . but that tackle stopped the game right there. I knew right then, that's what you have to do. That's not part of the game of football. How I felt that day, I was so proud of myself.

"I didn't get out of his way."

SOMETIMES, THE SECRET TO winning is not getting out of the bigger kid's way.

Fischer was willing to step up and tackle some of the most

feared football players of his day, even though he was giving up close to fifty pounds to many of them. But I have a feeling that it was that neighbor kid who hit him the hardest. And the ten-year-old Pat Fischer didn't flinch.

When you're not willing to back down—when you refuse to get out of the way—you become a problem for the other team. Your brand or your idea becomes something a giant has to navigate around, to plan for in advance. Your giant has to prepare a contingency plan when they know they stand a very real chance of having to deal with you out in the field, in front of the public. And when you've got better cards than your giant does, this works to your advantage.

What constitutes "being better"? In most situations, a vague term like "better" is very subjective. Even in supposedly objective areas, where simple us-versus-them measurement of a specific feature or performance level should answer the question, the clever and thoughtful strategist can find room for interpretation. After all, is it a problem when the upstart is "cheaper" when we have such superior service levels? Do we really have to deal with their "more capacity" when we are so much more reliable? And don't get me started on "taste," which is anyone's guess.

Let me just give you the answer here, because on this, there is no subjectivity. You're better when "they" say you are.

They, them, those people out there in the buying public—these are the people who need to believe your point. Regardless of whether you are working in the realm of objectivity or subjectivity, you need "them" to agree with you.

Why? Isn't my fact-based, evidence-steeped argument enough? No, and here's why. First, we're jaded. We distrust authority figures, even when they've got solid credentials. The rise of the vulgate—from Amazon reviews, to the blogosphere, to Yelp, to YouTube—has given us so many more sources of information in our decision making. Yes, we still trust the word of doctors, but this is now tempered with what we know from WebMD, what we know of the health care industry in general, whether our doctor made *Washingtonian Magazine*'s "Top Doctors" in his or her category of expertise, and how closely we've followed *House M.D.* on television.

Second, we're bombarded with too many messages. Depending on your source, we are hit with anywhere from a thousand to ten thousand marketing messages a day. This doesn't make us better consumers; it makes us numb. Our psychological walls are built so high at this point that we look for any shortcut we can find to sip from the fire hose of data. We "satisfice," a mashup of "satisfy" and "suffice," which describes what we do when we make decisions based on expediency, going for the "good enough" rather than determining what's optimal. We cut lots of corners in this process. I'm not saying it's correct and good, I'm just saying it is.

So when we talk about being "better" we need more than hyperbole. We need something defendable—something that lets us say, "Here's how you know we're the best."

The People's Choice: Cott Corporation

Cott did change the rules of the game . . . we were able to take a product up against two of the most powerful brands in the world, in a business where customers drink with their eyes.

—EDMUND O'KEEFFE, VICE PRESIDENT OF STRATEGY, COTT CORPORATION, AND PRESIDENT OF ROYAL CROWN INTERNATIONAL

Today, if you're in Canada, you can't miss Cott beverage products—President's Choice cola and a long list of other private-label retailer-owned soft drinks have a large foothold in the domestic market. In the 1990s, Coca-Cola and Pepsi were also very much aware of Cott's growing presence and followed the company's success with concern. Cott was a thorn in the sides of these two giants, prying away nearly a third of Canada's soft drink market share with a combination of operational leverage, the right product formulation, and aggressive marketing.

From its roots as a small, regional soft drink bottler serving the greater Quebec market, Cott emerged in the early 1990s as a serious threat to the established order of major brands with a well-constructed private-label strategy: a high-quality product, an improved margin to the retailers, a lower retail price to the consumer, and a promotional calendar to drive sell-through.

Edmund O'Keeffe, Cott's vice president of strategy, gave me an insider's perspective on how the company set out to disrupt the cola business. "Cott was changing the rules of the game, having a great quality product—a disruptive technology analogy, really—and then creating value so the retailer made more profit. The retailer could build a brand across the store and still be able to link in with the whole value brand phenomenon of being able to offer more to the customer." Cott's emergence coincided with a general consolidation of grocery retail in the early 1990s, with the relative balance of power moving toward the retailer and away from the brands. Thus, the prospect of a strong private-label supplier providing more than generic, "just good enough" product— including marketing support—was an attractive proposition.

In the late 1980s, the father of the modern Cott, Gerry Pencer, went to Loblaw, Canada's largest supermarket chain, and pitched them on a private-label cola strategy. David Nichol, the CEO of Loblaw, told Pencer that if he could provide them with a cola as good as Coke and Pepsi, then they'd get the business. Gerry, being the entrepreneur, agreed without actually knowing how he was going to deliver on this tall order. "Pencer went down to John Carson, who was running RC at the time, and negotiated to take over the excess capacity of RC Cola at their manufacturing cost," former NutraSweet president Rick Darnaby told me, relating his discussions with the early Cott team through his role as supplier of their aspartame sweetener. The choice of RC Cola as a formula and capacity provider wasn't by accident, either. "When we did taste tests on our drinks, as a general rule, RC Cola did the best, Pepsi came in second, and Coke came in third. And these were sip tests, which tend to favor sweeter drinks. So now they've got a product that wins most of the taste tests right off the bat."

All of a sudden, Cott had a product that not only was a blind taste-test winner but was available to him at a price that allowed margin both for it and for the retailer. For a retailer to be able to turn to a private-label brand for this kind of value was unique. With its operational and product strategy in hand, the company focused on signing private-label deals with major grocery chains across first Canada and then the United States with a two-pronged messaging strategy aimed at both the channel buyers and the consumers, exhorting both to "stop paying the brand tax." As O'Keeffe described it, "If you can't taste the difference, don't pay the difference."

In short order, Cott had signed up more than fifty private-label contracts with retailers in the United States and Canada, leveraging its stronghold in its original retail outlet, Canada's Loblaw, to penetrate the likes of Walmart and others.

How was it that a private-label brand could successfully and credibly take on two of the world's most powerful brands head to head—and not just compete but in many cases, win? We can look to several key components of their strategy. The company's operational structure gave them a strong cost position and the strategic maneuverability to give advantageous pricing to its grocery partners, and you can win a lot of fights if you're the brand that gives more gross margin to your channel. And its formulation and its product quality by virtue of its RC Cola relationship made it impossible to dismiss the brand's product quality.

The brand's "emperor has no clothes" rallying cry, pointing out the obvious disparity in price for a product as good as or better than the market leader resonated with both channel and value consumer. Retailers could make a higher margin on Cott products—often double what they could get from the major players. Supporting this pricing advantage was an in-house marketing organization that managed all aspects of promotion and merchandising for the brand, from advertising to trade promotion, giving the grocery customer a full-service experience at a private-label price. And, as Cott's O'Keeffe explained, this is a category "where customers drink with their eyes." Brand preference doesn't line up with taste-test results. So pulling the covers off the difference in taste and offering it for less money in a brand that deliberately positioned itself as private-label and budget-oriented struck home with many consumers. By the mid-1990s, Cott private-label brands had achieved the top spot in both Loblaw and Walmart.

What enduring lessons can we take away from Cott?

- **WHEN YOU'VE GOT A RELATIVE ADVANTAGE, SHOUT IT EARLY AND OFTEN.** Cott wasn't shy about calling out the major brands and their "brand tax." With long-term contracts in place and their operational side locked down, plus a formulation they knew was not just accepted but preferred by many of their customers, they could be as aggressive as they wanted with their messaging.

- **GIVE THE ELEPHANT IN THE ROOM A CATCHY AND UNFORTUNATE NICKNAME.** Sometimes we find ourselves in a situation where the truth is hanging in the air and no one seems to want to say it. There is real power in articulating what everybody else is thinking. When you say, "Don't pay the brand tax," you're giving voice to what we all intuitively know—that the giant's product is mostly sugar and water.

- **SOMETIMES, WHEN YOU SEEK TO KILL A GIANT, YOU OFTEN END UP KILLING ALL THE OTHER CHALLENGERS INSTEAD.** And that's fine, too. Did Cott look and act like a small private-label supplier? They had an in-house design and marketing agency and a distribution footprint that ran from Texas to the Arctic. They were bigger and better than any other private-label player while still a nimble brand to do business with.

Cott gives us a solid example of a "brand"—if we can call a collection of private-label brands a "brand"—that has successfully taken on two of the most powerful consumer branded franchises in the world, Coca-Cola and Pepsi, and succeeded in carving out a sustainable niche for itself through operational efficiencies, product quality, and a rallying cry that strongly resonates with channel and consumer alike.

My Facts Beat Your Feelings: Dunkin' Donuts

We sell more drip coffee than anyone else in this country. I'm going to repeat that. We sell more drip coffee than anyone else in this country. And we're only in 35 percent of it. We watched the coffee wars play out between Starbucks and McDonald's, which rankled. We also watched Howard Schultz having the effrontery to call our coffee swill. Add that to the list.

—FRANCES ALLEN, FORMER BRAND MARKETING OFFICER, DUNKIN' DONUTS

Imagine being the biggest player in your industry, only to have someone else claim to be the winner. Imagine other competitors entering the fray and battling the pretender for market supremacy—while you fight to be in the discussion. If this seems almost impossible to imagine, welcome to Frances Allen's world at Dunkin' Donuts. You feel like raising your voice and saying, "I'm right here, you know!" But why raise your voice when you can let the big, wide market of coffee drinkers raise their voices and defend you instead?

"I saw the success of the Pepsi Challenge," Allen told me, relating her previous experience at Pepsi as a vice president of marketing. "As a marketer, one of the beauties of switching industries is that you get to reinvent good ideas. That fresh thinking and naïveté means you're not hampered by history."

Let's take a moment to understand the company's spot in the American coffee market. "Dunkin' has been selling coffee for sixty years, so it's always been a part of the brand," Allen told me. "Another part of the brand is having the highest quality coffee. We've been buying the best quality beans for so many years that the growers call the highest quality beans DDQ—good enough for Dunkin' Donuts." Coffee, in other words, has always been important to Dunkin' Donuts and is a category worth defending. "Getting that ritual going—where the everyday visit is part of their routine—has been part of the strategy for a long time."

Against this backdrop, Starbucks emerged in the mid-1990s as the perceived quality leader, bringing a European-style roast coffee as well as its vaunted "third place" brand positioning— Starbucks offered an in-store experience that gave customers a place other than work or home where you could relax, be productive, listen to music, and enjoy coffee. Fast forward to 2007, and we saw the outbreak of the first hostilities in the now infamous "coffee wars," with behemoth McDonald's launching its McCafé branded stores and taking on the leaders in the business with its own version of premium coffee. Dunkin' could only watch with a sense of the surreal.

In 2008, the genesis of what was to become "Dunkin' Beats Starbucks" was conceived, with the Pepsi Challenge as the playbook. Allen's plan was to launch a campaign comparing Dunkin' coffee to Starbucks not just in the 35 percent of the country where Dunkin' franchises were located, but everywhere— even in markets where Dunkin' had no stores—including the Starbucks hometown of Seattle, Washington.

"We took on Starbucks because they were the perceived coffee leader," Allen explained. "When you design a test like this, it has to be conducted by an independent third party, it has to be fair, and it has to be defendable in a court of law. We had to brew the coffee using each brand's recommended equipment. You have to make sure it's bulletproof." When the test results came in, six out of ten coffee drinkers who expressed a preference said they preferred Dunkin'.

The campaign launched in 2008 under the umbrella of "America Runs on Dunkin'," with television, online, and other elements supporting the test results. Not only did the campaign position Dunkin' as a preferred brand against the perceived quality leader to coffee drinkers, it helped boost visibility and morale across the company's franchisees and was quickly picked up by the media. Consumers agreed. According to Mark Nunnelly, managing director at Bain Capital and a Dunkin' board member, Dunkin's share of the coffee market continued to steadily grow following the campaign despite the additional competition from both Starbucks and McDonalds.

Note the critical difference between this campaign and the Pepsi Challenge. I discussed the latter at length with former Coca-Cola chief marketing officer Sergio Zyman, and he was emphatic about what made that campaign work. "The interesting thing about the Pepsi Challenge was that it never claimed to taste better than Coke," he told me. "The great insight that we found out was that if you cross the line and start making superiority claims, the consumer is going to throw you out. The Pepsi Challenge was only intended to make Pepsi equal with Coke— not superior, because superior would not have been credible."

The Pepsi Challenge, in other words, never set out to prove head to head that Pepsi was better. The brilliance of the campaign strategy was in the showing, not the telling. Zyman emphasized this point, telling me, "The thing that was creating the wow factor was that when you removed the box that was hiding the two cans, the Coke drinker—who looked like a Coke drinker—would say, 'Oh my God, I can't believe it' . . . and then, they had the great line, which was, 'Don't take my word for it—let your taste decide.' "

While both campaigns were based on source similarity—that many people, like you, liked the favored brand—the Pepsi Challenge never said it was better. It said that you owe it to yourself to try this other product, because others like you liked it better. Be your own judge. Let your taste decide. Dunkin', on the other hand, relied on a rigorous statistical field study, as Allen described, showing actors portraying the various walks of life of the coffee market, stating that Dunkin' coffee was, in fact, the preferred brand. The meaning behind the words "Dunkin' Beats Starbucks" is fundamentally different than "the Pepsi Challenge."

"Taking on two huge giants like McDonald's and Starbucks with our coffee messaging was a brave step," Allen told me. "Doing a taste test was a brave step. I was just so confident in the quality of our products. Marketers have to take risks. Well-informed, calculated risks. That's what marketers need to do to cut through today's clutter and get their message heard."

What enduring lessons can we take away from Dunkin' Donuts and the "Dunkin' Beats Starbucks" Campaign?

- **YOU'RE BETTER WHEN "THEY" SAY YOU ARE.** Touting your superiority is a tricky thing, as Sergio reminds us above. You're better when they say you are—they, them, those people out there who buy your products and are just like everyone else who buys your products. Winning the war for the customer's devotion cures a lot of ills. But when you can claim this as yours, it's the best possible validation.

- **IT'S EVEN MORE POWERFUL WHEN THEY SHOW YOU HOW MUCH BETTER YOU ARE.** We communicate so much more than just our words when we talk face to face. Showing is more powerful than telling. If your market can identify with those who chose your cola or coffee—if they see people they relate to choosing you—they often will convince themselves that you're OK for them, too.

- **WHEN YOU HAVE THE FACTS, POUND THE FACTS.** In a world of subjectivity—even when we're doing a "taste test," the ultimate expression of subjectivity—we still cling to unarguable facts. Dunkin' had facts that reminded those consumers that didn't have a deeply held preference that Dunkin' really did make great coffee—and that others, like them, preferred Dunkin' to Starbucks. And back to their stores they went. Pepsi created doubt in the minds of die-hard Coke drinkers that maybe, perhaps, Pepsi wasn't necessarily an unacceptable choice.

Dunkin' Donuts provides us with a modern-day example of winning head to head using facts. Allen describes a campaign that clearly took the likely biases into account and went the extra mile to compare themselves to the perceived leader even in geographies where Dunkin' was at a competitive disadvantage by not having any stores. And with six out of ten people who expressed a preference going for their coffee, they had a rock-solid foundation to build out the rest of their campaign.

Killing Both Birds with One Stone:
SyQuest

We knew that the Zip drive was successful, and we postulated that it was partially due to the price point. So we decided to come out with a gigabyte drive at the same price.

—ED HARPER, FORMER CEO OF SYQUEST

The SyQuest story doesn't have a happy ending, a significant exception in this book. As I said at the beginning, I didn't set out to anoint "winners" here, only to identify strategies that were right for their time and place and from which the careful reader can learn valuable lessons. SyQuest, given this disclaimer, belongs in this discussion because they struck off in a direction that would have ultimately put the giant in their industry, Iomega, on its heels for an extended period of time. SyQuest had a breakout in its last gasps of life during that tumultuous period in technology toward the end of the 1990s, one that holds lessons for the careful student of business.

In 1997, Iomega was a giant in the world of removable data storage devices. Growing from $140 million in revenue prior to their launch of the wildly successful 100-megabyte Zip drive, they ballooned to more than $1.4 billion by 1997. Having traded leadership positions more than once with SyQuest, Iomega dedicated itself to finishing off its competitor once and for all with a program they dubbed GO, which stood for "game over." The company launched four Super Bowl ads the following January and went as far as buying the store fixtures upon which their product was merchandised in an attempt to ensure that they had the most prominent merchandising and signage in stores. They had, in so many words, more money than they knew what to do with. And with a smart brand identity and campaign, Iomega was poised to finally knock SyQuest down for good.

SyQuest had been a giant itself in the early nineties, with its 1.5 gigabyte SyJet drive being an industry standard for large file transportation. Graphic artists and engineers with complex CAD drawings didn't have the luxury of e-mailing their work to each other—the files were far too large for the early Internet. SyQuest's small, removable hard drives created a new category—until Iomega's Zip drive came along in 1994. With its decidedly smaller 100-megabyte storage capacity and much smaller price tag of roughly $199 for the drive and $20 for the removable disks, the Zip was a runaway hit. By 1996, SyQuest's imminent demise was predicted by many industry watchers.

"When I was recruited to come in, we had about $300 million in inventory in the channel that really had no home," former CEO Ed Harper told me. "At the time, the value-added resellers had stopped buying the stuff." Beyond an inventory problem and a disaffected channel, Harper faced a product suite that didn't make sense, not to mention a newly energized competitor with the wind at its back. Viewing his product portfolio, the current 1.5 gigabyte SyJet drive, against Iomega's offerings of the 100-megabyte Zip and 1-gigabyte Jaz drive, Harper felt the beginnings of a strategy take form. "We decided we'd take a middle approach, knowing that the Zip drive was very successful, and we postulated that it was partially due to the price point," Harper related. "We'd come out with a gigabyte drive at the same price. That's the drive that we came out with that really had an opportunity to take some of the wind out the sails of the Iomega product."

First, the company had to clean up a vast quantity of dead inventory and prepare the ground for the right product. The inventory in the channel was marked down and price protected to a lower price of $199 in concert with the launch of a rebranding campaign that took the company into uncharted territory. "The advertising campaign was designed to be very 'on the edge,' flirting with out-of-the-box ideas," Harper explained. Marketer Mike Smock was the consulting lead who worked on the corporate repositioning. "We had a limited amount of time to get sell-through up due to their precarious financial situation," Mike explained to me. "The value proposition was a small part of our positioning. The larger part was setting up a David-versus-Goliath conflict and using Iomega's energy and marketing budget to our advantage." The ad creative by Florent Wendling was, in fact, fairly risky for its day, and certainly positioned SyQuest as something more than a "speeds and feeds" marketer.

"We ran a full-page ad in the *New York Times* showing a Zip drive being tossed into a trash can," Smock told me, describing the first salvo in a compressed marketing campaign that had an estimated budget of $80 million. "We ran it knowing full well that Iomega would sue. We wanted Iomega to sue. We ran the ad, they issued a cease-and-desist letter, and we promoted their cease-and-desist letter. This led Herb Greenberg of the *San Francisco Chronicle* to write a column wondering what Iomega was afraid of and claiming that 'SyQuest is back!' His column had an enormous impact on the morale of the SyQuest troops and their channel partners." Sell-through had increased fivefold in a sixty-day timeframe and the stock had tripled.

The repositioning campaign prepared the market and the channel for the launch of SyQuest's long-awaited "Zip Killer" product, called the SparQ—a 1-gigabyte drive priced at $199, with the storage capacity of Iomega's larger Jaz drive priced at parity with its wildly popular Zip drive. The new drive, riding a wave of new momentum from Wall Street and consumer demand, was announced at the largest trade show of the industry, Comdex, in 1997 to rave reviews. Soon, the company was faced with the largest product backlog in its history. Three months later, Iomega reported a quarterly loss that it attributed to sales lost to the

SparQ drive. Iomega's CEO shortly thereafter was let go. Momentum had decidedly swung for the company many thought would cease operations just a few short months before.

"Had we been able to stick around for a little while, we would have had success with the SparQ drive," Harper told me in retrospect. How did this high-flying company fall to earth so quickly after such a dramatic run-up? Moments from victory, in what Harper confided was perhaps one quarter away from becoming cash-flow positive, the company's previous financing decisions caught up with them and they simply ran out of gas. "We had pushed financing to the very limit with Series S financing. We raised over $150 million from the bank, our vendors, and from investors as well. We just ran out of the ability to raise more money. We were one quarter away from a 'turn the corner' event for the company."

The company ceased operations late in 1998 and shortly thereafter declared bankruptcy, selling off its assets to its competitor, Iomega.

What enduring lessons can we learn from SyQuest?

- **IT'S HARD TO POSITION YOURSELF EFFECTIVELY AGAINST A COMPANY THAT MATCHES YOUR PRODUCT LINE, BEST FEATURE FOR BEST FEATURE.** SparQ had the storage capacity of the Jaz drive at the price of the Zip drive. Or, said another way, it had ten times the capacity of Zip for less than half the price of the Jaz. Take your pick, this product tied Iomega in knots.

- **DRIVE HOME THE ADVANTAGE, EARLY AND OFTEN.** When you've got a relative advantage in a fast-moving marketplace, drive the point home. SyQuest did this, spending $160 million between its advertising and its channel clean-up costs. Had it not been faced with cleaning up so much dead inventory in the channel, it might have saved enough on this campaign to see it through that last quarter and to break even.

- **THE BEST OPPONENT TO FACE IS HUBRIS.** Iomega was slow to react to the SparQ launch, and saw its Zip drive inventories climb and revenues fall, for one significant reason. The company simply felt it didn't have to react. Insiders knew there was a problem, but the hubris ran deep. Iomega had no answer for the SparQ drive but, luckily for them, time was running out on SyQuest.

- **NEVER WAIT TO MAKE THE DECISION YOU KNOW YOU'LL HAVE TO MAKE.** Ed Harper's final word on his SyQuest days tells a story in itself: "It was our mistake as managers that we took as long as we did to take the steps that we did. What we should have done would have been to cut it way back with the intention of starting it again with the SyJet and SparQ pair. We should have moved faster."

- **IT'S NEVER JUST ABOUT THE MARKETING.** Viewed against the backdrop of a host of other competitive strategy stories and lessons, this statement may feel out of place, but clearly it's not. SyQuest's breakout was a result of launching the right product positioned where it hurt the most together with an aggressive marketing campaign and significant channel investments to create interest and momentum. All three were necessary to achieve lift-off. And even this wasn't enough, ultimately. But, regardless of SyQuest's untimely end, this last gasp breakout holds a number of lessons for the careful reader.

SyQuest gives us an educational—and cautionary—story of a brand that successfully positioned the right product directly between its competitor's main two products, driving home the head-to-head comparison. SparQ was a Zip killer and certainly caused significant problems for Iomega during this brief period of time. Further, it was heavily promoted through national advertising, public relations, and channel initiatives. The company did a lot of things right. Ultimately, cash flow is the oxygen of all companies, and SyQuest's inability to raise more money for those last months before the anticipated break-even point did the company in.

Key Takeaways

As a smart brand, you know to **Show Your Teeth** when you have clear, competitive points of advantage—you promote these advantages to core stakeholders early and often. What key takeaways can we extract from these companies?

Consumer pull cures all ills. If your customers say you're better than the other guy, it doesn't really matter if the experts disagree or if there are a few dissenting opinions here and there. Customers are the ones who buy everything, and their vote is more important than everyone else's. Look at Dunkin'. Donuts. They statistically showed that coffee drinkers who had a preference preferred Dunkin'.

If you don't have all the facts on your side, you can still make your point—it's just a different point. The Pepsi Challenge is a terrific example of a campaign that simply suggests that your brand belongs in consideration. Pepsi never claims product superiority. And a picture tells a thousand words. When we let our customers see themselves in our advertising, we allow peers to sell other peers. This is always the most powerful way to convince a skeptical market, particularly in subjective areas.

Battles are often won and lost in the trenches of the channel. For channel-based businesses, being the partner of preference means you will be put in front of potential customers more often than the other guy. You will be an easy choice for customers who don't have a firm preference. And if your product works up to expectations, you might become a brand of choice as a result. Look at Cott. They show us a great example of delivering a quality product—in the eyes of the consumer—but at a price that allowed the retailer to make money. In the retailer's eyes, this means they can promote Cott heavily without incurring the wrath of their shoppers. If you can win in the soft drink aisle, or at the reseller level, or in the minds of your independent field sales representatives, you've done well.

You're better when you're bigger than their big guy and faster than their fast guy. Being better on multiple objective criteria is a hard one to beat when you're aiming to topple a giant. If you have clear objective criteria that say you're bigger, better, faster, and stronger than your competition, you're better. SyQuest had Iomega over a barrel with the SparQ drive and would have changed the face of the removable storage industry had it not run into other problems.

Splitting the giant's product line with a category killer product that does what their top two products do is a lesson we can learn from SyQuest.

When you're better, don't be shy about it. In all of these cases, we see the strategy come together and then the results aggressively pushed out to the market. When you're better, say so early and often, in every possible communications medium and industry forum.

CHAPTER ELEVEN: *Lessons, Big Ideas, and Where to Go from Here*

Killing giants is a complex business. Any time you find yourself competing for scarce resources in a market with an opponent who outweighs you, a head-to-head pushing match is the last thing you can afford to do. Fortunately, we've discussed thirty-three different stories and ten different strategies that illustrate how smart thinking and the careful application of leverage can put the giant on its back.

It's not easy. It's never easy to do anything as monumental as defeating a major competitor. That's what makes this discussion so interesting.

Let's look at what we've covered from a different angle now. We've discussed specifics around these ten strategies and illustrated how many nimble companies have outmaneuvered giants, but squint and look across these chapters and a number of trends emerge. The act of competing with brains instead of brawn lends itself to certain observations that cut across these chapters horizontally and hold a few lessons that will help us better explore these in-between spaces.

What are the big takeaways we can derive when we consider all of these chapters together?

Lessons

#1.
Giants have different problems than you do.

We heard from Jim Koch at the Boston Beer Company, Herman Mashaba at Black Like Me, Eric Ryan at Method, and others that the giant couldn't really do what they do because, once a company reaches a critical mass of size, they have different problems. Brands stop focusing on being good at what made them great and start being great at making much more of what they make. They're no longer a master brewer; they're a supply chain company.

This insight is important. I put this question to each entrepreneur I spoke to because I was genuinely interested in understanding how they took this plunge. Couldn't the giant in their industry just squash them if they wanted to? Well, yes, but . . . they can't. Anheuser-Busch technically could retool their breweries to do what Samuel Adams beer does, but they won't. It isn't worth it to them. It would take up too much of their attention and time for too little a gain.

Could a Revlon have competed head to head against Black Like Me in the townships of South Africa given the right products, naming strategies, and local marketing? Perhaps. But what we're describing really isn't the way a global competitor fights, is it?

The same idea holds true with Baidu in China, as well. Could Google have really competed on a head-to-head basis the way Baidu competed in China? Yes, but. It just isn't how the company operates.

Look at Method and you see a similar story. The Procter & Gambles of the world don't want their brand managers focusing this intently on developing that much expertise in a finite space. Their job is to do well and get promoted in eighteen months to another, bigger job. This doesn't lend itself to accumulating the expertise that Jim Koch calls "getting it under your fingernails." Now we understand why Koichi Kimura of Miki House specifically discusses the "optimal size of a company."

This should be an epiphany for anyone cautiously dipping their toe in the pool and wondering if the giant lurking beneath the surface will swallow them whole. I'm not saying that there's no risk in launching a new company in a space dominated by a giant. But I am saying that a very interesting group of people here have pointed out that just because you share a market doesn't mean you'll be their biggest concern. Adding 1 percent more volume to their largest customer is far more important to them than spending the time and effort duplicating what a startup is trying to do.

Given the words of advice that we've heard from these industry luminaries in these far-flung fields, it's fair to say that a lot of your success is going to come down to how you do what you do and not just what.

#2.

Giants can't go where you go anymore.

It's been said that over time, people start looking a lot like their dogs. Companies are like this, too. They begin to coalesce around certain principles and practices that define their space. The longer a company is successful, the less they feel the need to revisit how they do what they do. Consumers, for their part, build up a certain set of expectations of what is acceptable and what is perfectly fine to live without. And this is a lethal blind spot.

Look at the stories we've discussed that show how smart brands have done things their giant competitors find impossible or unthinkable. Prizeotel doesn't even have a phone in the room! No minibar? You prepay when you check in? What? This isn't a hotel! It's a vending machine! Exactly. Marco Nussbaum has deconstructed everything we've come to expect about a hotel and given us exactly what we want instead. Vibram and their FiveFingers running shoe gives us a story about a product so different that it would cause a typical giant to throw out everything it stood for, were they to try to launch a similar product. Miki House tells us that no, it isn't OK to make substandard products just because our children will outgrow them before they're worn out. What? Impossible! 42Below refuses to be a corporate suit. You can't say that! But they did. Xfire and Mike Cassidy were launching new products while their competitors were still arranging their task forces to evaluate his last idea. Cricket does what no other advertising agency would dream of doing, not because its competitors couldn't—but because its competitors never thought they'd have to. Look at WellDyne and their elimination of fiefdoms, silos, and bureaucracy. These are the things their competitors work for their whole professional lives. Losing these perks wouldn't go over well. So Damien Lamendola made the choice easy by providing the right culture up front.

Giants don't just grow up. They grow into habits, structures, and expectations. This is an opportunity for reinvention. And it isn't just for entrepreneurs, either.

#3.
The rest never takes care of itself.

Giants, by their very nature, have more dollars than time. This is a function of their rewards systems as much as anything. The habits they come by are borne of this desire to quickly move on: on to the next project, the next brand, the next promotion. Often, when faced with big moving parts and overlapping agencies (that also have their own rewards systems in place, let's not forget), we see the tendency to assume at a certain point that "the rest will take care of itself." The ad campaign is in the can, the press tour is underway . . . what could go wrong?

The rest never takes care of itself, and when left to chance—and when faced with a nimble, smart, and aggressive competitor—this is when and where and how million-dollar ideas blow up.

Look at the examples of companies that have stepped in and taken control of the dialogue after the giant's attention has waned. Go Daddy realized that they needed to take the reins in their own hands and make sure everybody—*everybody*—knew that they could buy a domain name for themselves. Adobe tactically stepped in between its primary competitor and the ad it knew it had in its hands and walked away with a Black Friday coup. Fiskars stepped in with a passionate team of evangelists and made the no-name cost-driven nonbrands a nonfactor. Classe made sure that their channel salespeople burned with passion and expertise for their products. Intuit built a culture that brought the customer into the boardroom, quickly ending internal debate and delivering on customer needs faster and more accurately than its competitors because it knew—with hard evidence—what it needed to do. Belkin embedded itself into the retail planogram like a tick, understanding the intricacies of space management in far more detail than its competitors ever could. Indium speaks to its customers in a voice and with the gravity that its competitors can't hope to match. Tab Clear didn't give Crystal Pepsi any breathing room, attaching itself to this massive product launch and bringing both of them down. JetBlue practically gives extra seats away—and if it didn't ensure that every flight delivered on its promise to "bring humanity back to air travel," this strategy would backfire. But they do, so it doesn't. iProspect's campaign for Oslo University shouldn't have worked—but their competitor left the door open for an online search campaign, stealing the giant's eyeballs and prospective students.

The rest didn't take care of itself. You can't just rely on the

IT department spreading the word, or the ad doing its job, the hot price winning over the customer, or the big trade show booth swaying your client's buying decisions. In each of these cases, covering both entrepreneurs as well as companies that have been operating for hundreds of years, we see the ability to step beyond the obvious and get closer to the needs of the market, face to face, and deliver when everyone else has incorrectly assumed the job was done.

#4.

Inspiration always comes from elsewhere.

The next time you need inspiration, go for a long walk.

Studying other industries in other countries at both the strategic and the tactical levels allows you to temporarily try on alternate realities from which you can see your world in a new light. Think of Dr. Steven Feinberg's idea of "strategic shifting"—go climb a mountain and view your battlefield from a different perspective, preferably one your opponent has yet to fully grasp.

Jim Koch wanted to change how Americans thought about beer, and he took his inspiration from the American wine industry. Eric Ryan of Method said his brand was "Aveda for the home," connecting personal care and health and beauty aids to the detergent category. Herman Mashaba's Black Like Me was designed to be "the Coca-Cola of cosmetics," available everywhere throughout the townships of South Africa. Vibram's FiveFingers athletic shoe actually did come from elsewhere—from an Italian designer working on a thesis—and the combination of his brilliant and unorthodox idea with Vibram's cultural heritage and innovative culture created a category. Oi Mobile's inspiration came from Orange, another carrier, albeit on a different continent. Zipcar's inspiration came from Europe but was shaped by a confluence of other societal and technological trends.

Whether the spark of the idea comes from another industry you've observed or is merely a metaphor, these companies have often taken what's worked elsewhere and skillfully applied it to their own situations.

#5.

Giants don't like to fight—especially against you.

Nobody likes surprises. Nobody likes to be forced to compete when they've got other things on their to-do list. We like the personal freedom to make our own choices and to put our plans in motion based on our own timetables—and giant-killers mess things up by laying down challenges that giants didn't anticipate and see no glory in winning.

When a giant is forced to face off against an upstart brand, like our giant-killers here, there is virtually no upside in winning—but the downside is severe. Losing is a catastrophe for a giant. The upstart, however, has nothing but upside. They're not really supposed to win, are they? This asymmetrical game of chicken is ideal for the underdog. The giant is on the dais, delivering its prepared speech, and you're in the audience, heckling away.

Look at Tab Clear during Crystal Pepsi's launch. Pepsi couldn't shake Tab off its shoes fast enough. The other soft drink story, Cott Beverages, also shows us an awkward brand to fight. The giant brands can't afford to compete on price, and they don't want to compete on quality because they stand a good chance of losing a taste test. Dunkin' was a similarly inconvenient fight for Starbucks because Starbucks was gearing up to fight McDonald's. Cricket's performance-based business model brings up a conversation the ad agency world doesn't want to discuss.

From your perspective, the giant may be big enough to step on you. From their perspective, you're the urchin they fear to tread on.

#6.

Creating the perfect, self-defining storm

Do you know what an eigenvalue is?

"This sentence has five words." That's an eigenvalue—a self-defining truism, something unarguable. Its representation is its definition.

The concept of the eigenvalue is borrowed from the field of cybernetics, and it has influenced such far-flung disciplines as philosophy, psychology, architecture, and art. It belongs in your playbook, as well, because the more we look across the sweep of these stories, the more we see examples of smart, nimble brands doing something that only they could pull off.

When Koichi Kimura tells us that, "Everything comes from the same idea of doing what's in children's best interests," he tells us that everything Miki House does is self-referencing, from its product designs to its new business development activities in education and sports sponsorships. No shoe company could have introduced the FiveFingers, but a brand known for innovation in the shoe sole business could. Now, the story would be credible and authentic. When Marty St. George says he wants customers to say, "This could only come from JetBlue," he's telling us he views the world through this eigenvalue lens. Could a global cosmetics giant credibly launch a brand in the townships of South Africa during apartheid called Black Like Me? Unlikely. Oi Mobile launched with a promotion offering thirty-one years of free weekend-to-weekend calling—thirty-one being their initial coverage area's city code. A promotional eigenvalue.

We see examples of eigenvalues running through these companies like a thread. These brands, whether start-up or long established, understand that their uniqueness is their defining strength.

Creating the Right Toolbox
for Your New "Thinking Tools"

Some of the stories in *Killing Giants* won't apply to your situation. Others are dead-on. One or more have pushed you off-balance, making you think about things in a different way. Let's focus on those for now.

Here's how I analyze stories and find ways to apply them to situations that might not look like they'd fit. I create diagnostic processes—think of them as "thinking tools"—that lead me to the same courses of action that the hero of my story did. I use this technique as a creative tool, and it often helps me get past my clients' (and my own) personal blinders.

Want to try this?

Let's pick **Winning in the Last Three Feet.** Here's one set of tools—there are more at KillingGiants.com.

Winning in the Last Three Feet requires that we understand how our customer makes decisions—where they look for information, what they value the most, and exactly when they will be committing their money.

We need to "attach ourselves to the order" and understand where it is at all times. Further, it requires a careful gap analysis between what our giant is spending their money on and where our opportunities may be. Let's see where this analysis takes us.

1. **IDENTIFY THE "TOUCH POINTS."** Start with a blank piece of paper and write down each and every step a customer takes in his or her interaction with your brand, from the first introduction to the end of product life. Don't forget that the experience you're looking to attach yourself to doesn't have to end with purchase. Start at the very beginning and take us to the very end.

Overlay both our giant's areas of strength and focus and our own. Where does the giant spend most of its time? If they're like most, the giant will play a big part in the early stages, because this is where the money is spent. Write down what the giant does in each of these stages.

What do our customers—and our giant's customers—think? Conduct in-depth one-on-one interviews with your customers and have them fill out what they recall about interacting with our giant's brand and our own. Question them specifically on whether they recall interacting with anyone on each of the stages you've identified. Ask them if there were other steps that you missed. Create a complete picture. What you as an insider think your customers perceive and what they tell you they remember are likely to be two very different pictures.

Who are the stakeholders—people who have a role in the customer's process during each "touch point"? Who are the gate-keepers—people who have to approve the purchase? At retail, that's often all the same person, walking into the store with wallet in hand—but in B2B, these may be a long list of people.

2. **STUDY THE GAPS.** Where is the giant weak? Where does it not participate? At which point do they assume the sale is made? Is this a point at which you can enter the conversation? Analyze these gaps carefully, alongside your customers if possible, and come up with ideas for how you can meaningfully enter the discussion.

Stop and ask yourself: At which point in the transaction is the customer open to suggestion? In a retail environment, this can happen when an "influencer" tells them there's something else they should consider—a retail salesperson, a display—and may happen at the point of purchase. In a B2B environment, this may be earlier in the process—in organic (or paid) search or the opinion of the CFO—and may take place in several different ways. Rate each step along the way based on your ability to convert the customer away from the alternative: Where are they open to a new suggestion and who is the most likely "influencer" to do this?

3. **CREATE NEW GAPS.** Can you create new "touch points" that you can brand and own? Now is the time to be creative, bringing those areas where you have the ability to influence the conversation to the foreground and where our giant is completely left out. Question the givens at this stage carefully. Often, what we assume is standard practice is only standard to us, not our customers.

4. **WHAT IS OUR MESSAGE?** Now that we've identified those "touch points" where our giant has left the side door open, what should we be saying? And who should be saying it? We may find that there are half a dozen ways we can leverage our giant's spending—or we may find only one door left open that makes the entire exercise worthwhile. But each requires a carefully developed intercept message. How do you craft your intercept message?

Are you actively fighting against a branded, acknowledged giant where the customer is going to have to pick you over them? If yes, understand you're starting with the assumption that the giant is the incumbent in the customer's mind and start from here.

What you say next in this "touch point" needs to answer the question, "Compared to what?"

The contrast phenomenon, as described in Dr. Robert Cialdini's book *Influence: Science and Practice*, teaches us that we can change how anyone perceives anything—so long as we control what they hear first, just before we make our request. Where do we compare favorably with our giant?

Are they more expensive? Do we offer more options? Do recognized experts prefer us? Instead of this, you can have that. Set yourself up for a favorable impression using the contrast phenomenon.

Try developing your intercept message using this concept of contrast. Write it down. Is there meaningful separation between our giant's proposition and what we offer? Rewrite it—this time with a more exaggerated degree of contrast. Try it again. Your third draft will help bring this into focus.

5. **MAKING IT A SURE THING**. We've identified those "moments of power" that matter, found the right gaps where we have a relative advantage, and now crafted the right message to deliver in that moment where the consumer is open to suggestion. What else can we do to slam the door on our giant?

Does this idea lead us to buying unique domain names that surround the consumer when they're looking for our solution? Do we put a more comprehensive educational training program around our channel salespeople because we see an opening there? Is there an additional offer that we can put in our consumers' hands at this point that solidifies the positioning we've taken in our messaging and pushes them further toward choosing us, not our giant?

What can we do in this spot to create more than just a relative advantage? How can we turn this gap into a defendable space?

6. **FINISH WELL**. Winning in the Last Three Feet is all about not leaving things to chance, not assuming that "the rest will take care of itself." So let's not fall prey to this same trap at the last moment ourselves. Let's ask ourselves, "What next?" What happens then? Then what? How does the chain of events—taken from your "touch points" through your intercept through your successful conversion of the sale—absolutely end? Let's

remind ourselves that it might not be over when the sale is made. As a matter of fact, let's make sure it doesn't.

Map out the specific implementation steps needed to make sure the customer is landed.

That's finishing well.

That's how I looked at **Winning in the Last Three Feet.** The idea of disaggregating an idea—of reverse-engineering a success story, in other words—is a powerful "thinking tool" and one that can help you extract meaning out of the stories you hear. Squint and you can see Adobe, Classe, and Fiskars in this analysis. The same applies to other examples.

I urge you to try this. Don't just read stories like these as literature. They contain real meaning and potentially an insight or two that can make a significant impact in your business.

Go to www.killinggiants.com/tools and download a similar "thinking tool" for **Thin Ice.**

Conclusions

Giants, as literary devices, have been cast as the bad guys here. It's understandable, but let me back away from this briefly as we close and offer up a new idea and hopefully put the idea of "giant-ness" back into our good graces.

If there is any specific spine to this entire story, it's this.

Ideas are powerful. They can transform our brands, our companies, and our careers in a way that money can't.

Ideas can make us "giants."

We can become something greater than the economic resources that are put in our care by others. The giant, in other words, lives within us. We just have to do what is necessary to uncover that spark, and often this means we must travel a path that others would rather avoid.

It's uncomfortable.

It's inconvenient.

It's so much easier to throw money instead.

But in order to break through and distill the greatness that our creativity and our passion and dedication to our art can become, we need to take this journey.

This is a hopeful message for anyone living a life of business. It's the story of how to become a giant, how to truly lead from wherever you are in your organization, at any level. This requires tapping in to the human spirit of creativity and curiosity and the desire that we all have. The brands that are truly great are the ones that are constantly looking for ways to deliver what their markets want—"just not the way the market expects to get it," to paraphrase screenwriter Robert McKee one last time. They don't just push stuff out on the marketplace. They listen and they engage and they find a way to stay true to their core while still managing to innovate and create and evolve and reinvent themselves.

It is a hopeful message to say that we can embrace constraints, fight giants, and win—because we are inspired by the stories of those who have gone out before us and have shared their experiences.

There is power in ideas. Now, to work!

Acknowledgments

What's the matter with you? Why haven't you written your book yet?"

To be honest, the ideas behind *Killing Giants* date back to my first blog post on the subject in 2007. But it took a drive over Highway 17 from my Santa Cruz, California, home turf to Palo Alto to grab a cup of coffee with Roger von Oech, author of *A Whack on the Side of the Head* and creator of the Creative Whack Pack, to snap me out of my blogging reverie.

Roger's push got me going. But anytime you go out and interview seventy-plus business leaders on every continent except Antarctica, you need to rely on people. And I had a lot of people, many of whom deserve a lot of credit for helping me on this journey.

My inner sanctum advisers, both in business and in writing *Killing Giants*, played significant roles in vastly different ways. Rick Darnaby provided immeasurable help in not only identifying and but also fleshing out a number of critical stories. Dr. Steven Feinberg provided me with not only his personal experience going down the path of authorship but also in very specific areas where the psychological angle of the thing told the story. He's interviewed at length in *Killing Giants,* but his contributions run like a thread throughout.

It took five rewrites of my proposal to grab Jim Levine's attention. Jim and his team at Levine Greenberg Literary Agency were worth the effort. He has overdelivered on every promise. The first conversation with the team at Portfolio convinced me I was in the right hands. "After reading your proposal, we now see that there's a gap in the current literature." Many thanks to David Moldawer for his guidance, excruciatingly detailed editing, and active participation in the development of the book and to Adrian Zackheim for taking the leap of faith on a first-time author.

As I said, many people nudged the project forward, from providing introductions to giving insights. These people, in no particular order, include Christina Kerley, Terry Lloyd, Ari Lopez, Bob Kron, Chris Archibald, Anne Friscia, Jessica Pearson, Dan Benjamin, Patti Lorin, Howie Lipstein, Tom Evans, Lonnie Arima, Yoshi Takeda, Lora Elder, Will Sarni, Andrew Winston, Bruce Ludemann, Setsuko Ogata, Fabio Vaninni, Byron Sage, Mandy de Waal, Bob Livingston, Misha Janette Flemming, the Stanford Entrepreneur's Forum, Jay Ehret, Anne Handley, Tony Gomez, Steve Woodruff, Bob Bertini, Marcella Zaiden, Tina Campbell, Martin Roll, Heather Anderson, Richard Lennon, Kriselle Laran, David Meerman Scott, Tom Asacker, Dan Pink, Amy Federman, Julie Weed, Tim Grahl, Stephanie Bracken, Elizabeth Driscoll, Stephanie Schweitzer, Yvonne Malmgren, Erin Stattel, Jeffrey Record, Paula Butler, Rainey Foster, my big brother Christopher, and sainted mother Susan Denny. For starters, at least.

My interviewees and their insights are the heart and soul of this effort. Again, in no particular order, I must thank Aaron Duran, Kaiser Kuo, Paulino Barros, Sally Jackson, Moky Makura, Spike Jones, Mike Smock, Karim Rashid, Dr. Christopher Meyer, Simon Young, Jim Koch, Robin Li, Herman Mashaba, Mandy

Torvick, David Nauber, Sander Alten, Robert Murray, Greg Fous, Bob Striano, Marty St. George, Scott Griffith, John Williams, Bob Parsons, Suzanne Fanning, Koichi Kimura, Ed Harper, Edmund O'Keeffe, Frances Allen, Sergio Zyman, Marco Nussbaum, Trudy Hardy, Jim McDowell, Geoff Ross, Rick Short, Steve Mullen, Richard Hinson, Eric Ryan, Dr. Edmund Schweitzer, Mark Reynoso, Scott Wilder, Damien Lamendola, Mike Cassidy, Rob Willington, Georgia Shaw, Tony Post, Maxim Medvedovsky, Victor Grillo, Bert Sugar, Victor Bazan, Tamsin Smith, Pat Fischer, Robert McKee, Dr. J. E. Lendon, Ole Schack, Paul Leinberger, Norman Holland, Paul Dibbayawan, Conrad Crane, and Bob Hamman.

Researching a book with thirty-three stories, told first-person, wouldn't have been possible in the deceptively short time period of two years without the networks and tools that make information available at any time of the day or night. The Marketing Executives Networking Group (MENG) was a source of inspiration and redirection more than once. And tools like Skype, LinkedIn, Twitter, MP3MyMP3, my Radio Shack Telephone Recording Controller, and Jungle Disk made it all possible, if not exactly effortless.

Last, for those of you who choose to go down the path of mining a story out of your own head, understand the role your family will play in the process. They have to live with you while all this is happening. The two a.m. calls to South Africa, the four a.m. calls to Brazil, the ideas that interrupt dinner, the conversations that keep circling back to that one problematic chapter, the games of catch that get delayed another fifteen minutes because the Muse isn't playing along right now—all these moments are commonplace for the better part of a year. Be prepared, but be thankful. It's fun in a painful, trying sort of way. To my (currently twelve-year-old) Director of Creativity, Nicholas, I appreciate absolutely every idea you've come up with and look forward to collaborating with you on future projects, great and small.

ACKNOWLEDGMENTS

To my (currently three-year-old) Management Trainee, Alexander, I'm never too busy to stop for a boisterous meeting in the middle of the day. And to my Vice President of Operations and "Associate Marketing Manager," Christine, you've been a greater support and source of constant inspiration than you'll ever know, just one more reason why I'm madly in love with you. In case you were wondering.

As my father, author Robert Denny, was fond of saying, "Bitsy bitsy swazo finishli," which he assured us meant, "Slowly, slowly, the bird builds its nest." *Killing Giants* has been that kind of journey. As to the language of origin of this now famous family saying, it remains shrouded in mystery.

Index

BRING ME IN TO SPEAK AT YOUR NEXT EVENT

A keynote address to your assembled troops can be one of the most effective ways of spreading the doctrine of brains over brawn. Whether you need someone to motivate your sales force, provide an executive briefing with your senior staff, or give your entire organization a new sense of what's possible in your highly competitive world, I can offer illuminating stories and practical advice on killing your particular giant.

Are your competitive challenges more complex? Would a half-day or day-long workshop help you and your team work through the various angles of attack? Let's discuss how a *Killing Giants* workshop can help you build on your current strategic and tactical plans.

You can contact me at **www.stephendenny.com** and on Twitter at **@Note_to_CMO.** I look forward to getting in touch.